Horace Walpole, John Long, George Coleman

Voyages and Travels of an Indian Interpreter and Trader

Vol. 1

Horace Walpole, John Long, George Coleman

Voyages and Travels of an Indian Interpreter and Trader
Vol. 1

ISBN/EAN: 9783337345761

Printed in Europe, USA, Canada, Australia, Japan

Cover: Foto ©Andreas Hilbeck / pixelio.de

More available books at **www.hansebooks.com**

VOYAGES AND TRAVELS

OF AN

INDIAN INTERPRETER AND TRADER,

DESCRIBING

The Manners and Customs

OF THE

NORTH AMERICAN INDIANS;

WITH

AN ACCOUNT OF THE POSTS

SITUATED ON

THE RIVER SAINT LAURENCE, LAKE ONTARIO, &c.

TO WHICH IS ADDED,

A VOCABULARY

OF

The Chippeway Language.

Names of Furs and Skins, in English and French.

A LIST OF WORDS

IN THE

IROQUOIS, MOHEGAN, SHAWANEE, AND ESQUIMEAUX TONGUES,

AND A TABLE, SHEWING

The Analogy between the Algonkin and Chippeway Languages.

BY J. LONG.

LONDON:

PRINTED FOR THE AUTHOR; AND SOLD BY ROBSON, BOND-STREET; DEBRETT, PICCADILLY; T. AND J. EGERTON, CHARING-CROSS; WHITE AND SON, FLEET-STREET; SEWELL, CORNHILL; EDWARDS, PALL-MALL; AND MESSRS. TAYLORS, HOLBORN, LONDON; FLETCHER, OXFORD; AND BULL, BATH.

M,DCC,XCI.

LIST OF SUBSCRIBERS.

Addis, Mr. George.
Annereau, Mr.

Banks, Sir Joseph, Bart.
Beaufoy, Henry, Esq. M. P.
Berens, Hermanus, Esq.
Berens, Joseph, Esq.
Boddam, Thomas, Esq.
Bettesworth, Thomas, Esq.
Baker, John, Esq.
Baker, William, Esq.
Baker, Miss.
Batson, Robert, Esq.
Baynes, Burdon, Esq.
Blache, J. F. Esq.
Belfour, John, Esq.
Belfour, Mr. Okey. 3 copies.
Belfour, Mr. J. D.
Bird, William, Esq.
Bird, Thomas, Esq.
Bird, Michael, Esq.
Barbe, St. Samuel, Esq.
Barbe, St. John, Esq.
Bingley, ———, jun. Esq.

Bates, Mr. John.
Birkley, Mr. John.
Bowden, John, Esq.
Brandon, Mr.
Bull, Mr. J. Bath.
Beilby, Mr. 6 copies.

Croft, the Rev. Herbert.
Cornthwaite, the Rev. Mr.
Chalmers, George, Esq.
Culverden, William, Esq.
Corsellis, Nicholas Cæsar, Esq.
Coussmaker, John, Esq.
Croix, N. D. St. Esq.
Cleaver, Miss.
Cotton, Thomas, Esq.
Cotton, Bayes, Esq.
Chandler, George, Esq.
Coningham, William, Esq.
Cope, Thomas, Esq.
Cleugh, John, Esq.
Clay, Felix, Esq.
Clay, James, Esq.
Clay, William, Esq.

iv LIST OF SUBSCRIBERS.

Clay, George, Esq.
Cooper, Mr.
Cooper, Mr. James.
Corbet, ——, Esq. 2 copies.

Dawson, William, Esq.
Dalrymple, Alexander, Esq.
Dicken, John, Esq.

Earle, James, Esq.
Emes, William, Esq.
Edwards, Charles, Esq.
Etches, R. C. Esq.
Eldridge, Thomas, Esq.

Fraser, Major.
Finch, Thomas, Esq.
Forbes, Thomas, Esq.
Fayle, Benjamin, Esq.
Faden, Mr. William. 6 copies.
Fawler, Mrs.
Forsteen, ——, Esq.
Finch, Mr. John.
Fletcher, Mr. James, Oxford.

Grote, George, Esq.
Gould, Thomas, Esq.
George, C. G. Esq.

Goldthwaite, Thomas, Esq.
George, Mr. Edward.
Graft, Mr. James.

Hollingsworth, John, Esq.
Hulse, Richard, Esq.
Hulse, Edward, Esq.
Howison, John, Esq. Lisbon.
Hayward, Francis, Esq. 2 copies.
Holden, Joseph, Esq.
Haffey, John, Esq.
Hill, Edward, Esq.
Hussey, William Wheatley, Esq.
Harper, Mrs.
Hillier, Mr.
Hale, Mr. Harry. 2 copies.
Hill, Mr. John.

Jones, Edward, Esq.
Jeudwine, Thomas, Esq.
Justice, Mr. Richard.
Jacks, Mr.

Knill, John, Esq.
Kensington, Charles, Esq.

Long, Sir James Tylney, Bart. M. P.
    7 copies.

LIST OF SUBSCRIBERS.

Lake, Sir J. Winter, Bart. 4 cop.
Langmore, William, Esq.
Legg, Leaver, Esq.
Long, Mrs.
Locke, Miss.
Locke, John, Esq.
Lion, Thomas, Esq.
Lane, Benjamin, Esq.
Lang, Charles, Esq.
Lightfoot, John, Esq.
Lonsdale, Mr.

Mulgrave, the Right Hon. Lord.
Monsel, Lieutenant Colonel.
Marsden, William, Esq.
Morris, John, Esq.
Martin, Captain.
Man, Henry, Esq. 6 copies.
Mukins, Francis, Esq.
Malleson, John, Esq.
Murray, Mr. J. 2 copies.

Nesbitt, Lieutenant Colonel.
Nesbitt, Arnold, Esq.
Nasmyth, Maxwell, Esq.
Neave, Richard, Esq.

Prescott, George William, Esq.

Pott, Rev. J. H. Archdeacon of
   St. Albans.
Pott, Percival, Esq.
Pott, E. H. Esq.
Pott, Mrs.
Powell, Baden, Esq.
Powell, James, Esq.
Powell, Thomas, Esq.
Peck, Jasper, Esq.
Pooley, John, Esq.
Perry, John, Esq.
Palmer, Peregrine, Esq.
Pickwoad, Robert, Esq,
Pickering, Thomas, Esq.
Popplewell, Mr.

Roberts, John Esq.
Rennell, Major.
Robertson, Captain.
Ruspini, J. B. Esq.
Rouse, Benjamin, Esq.
Ross, G. W. Esq. 2 copies.
Rutter, Miss.
Row, William, Esq.
Regail, Alexander, Esq.
Reading Society, Hackney.

Scott, Thomas, Esq. M. P.

A

LIST OF SUBSCRIBERS.

Sneyd, Samuel, Esq.
Symons, the Rev. Mr.
Sheldon, John, Esq. Professor of Anatomy in the Royal Academy of Arts, London, and F. R. S.
Shamier, ———, Esq.
Stoe, Harry, Esq.
Sedgwick, Harry, Esq.
Stone, John Hurford, Esq.
Surman, William, Esq.
Smith, Haskett, Esq.
Scafe, Mr. Richard.
Scargill, Mr. James.
Stable, Mr. William.
Smith, Mr. Thomas.
Smith, Mr. J. Thomas.

Turner, Miss.
Turner, Miss Jane.
Tanner, N. Esq.
Toulmin, William, Esq.

Taylors, Messrs. 6 copies.
Vaston, Mrs.
Vandriel, Mr. J. C.

Wegg, Samuel, Esq.
Winter, John, Esq.
Walker, John, Esq.
Wilson, Stephen, Esq.
Wilson, William, Esq.
Wilcox, William, Esq.
Wilcox, Edward, Esq.
Wilcox, Mrs. Anne.
Wickham, Lieut.
Woolhead, Major, Esq.
Wright, Mr. Thomas.
Watson, Mr. William.
White, Messrs. and Son. 6 copies.

Young, Mrs.

PREFACE.

THE reader will naturally expect some account of this work.

With regard to the historical part, I have endeavoured to explain the situation of the Posts, which, by Mr. Oswald's Treaty, were stipulated to be surrendered to the Americans; and pointed out their convenience to Great Britain in a political and commercial point of view: I have also given a description of the Five and Six Nation Indians; and endeavoured to shew the usefulness, as well as necessity, of a strict alliance with them as long as we retain any possessions in Canada.

With respect to the descriptions of lakes, rivers, &c. which lie beyond Lake Superior, from Lake Nipegon to Lake Arbitibis, I have given them as accurately as possible, either from my own knowledge, or the most authentic Indian accounts; and when it is considered that interpreters in the commercial line seldom have occasion for any geographical knowledge, the want of better information will be excused.

The Vocabulary which is subjoined, and on which I have bestowed some pains, it is hoped will not only afford information to such as may be desirous of attaining a knowledge of the Chippeway language, but prove useful to those who are already engaged in traffic with the Indians.

PREFACE.

As the mode of spelling a language which has never been reduced to a grammatical system, must be arbitrary, and principally depend on the ear, I have endeavoured to use such letters as best agree with the English pronunciation; avoiding a multiplicity of consonants, which only perplex: and to enable the reader to speak so as to be understood by the natives, it is necessary to observe that *a* is generally sounded broad; and *e* final never pronounced but in monosyllables.

The following are the motives which induced me to make the Vocabulary in the Chippeway language so copious.

In the first place it is, strictly speaking, one of the mother tongues of North America, and universally spoken in council by the chiefs who reside about the great lakes, to the westward of the banks of the Mississippi, as far south as the Ohio, and as far north as Hudson's Bay; notwithstanding many of the tribes, within the space of territory I have described, speak in common a different language.—This observation is confirmed by authors of established repute, and further proved by the concurrent testimony of the Indian interpreters.

Baron de Lahontan asserts that the Algonkin is a mother tongue, and that it is in as much estimation in North America, as Greek and Latin in Europe: this being admitted, I am persuaded the Chippeway language possesses as much, if not greater merit, as it is in every respect better understood by the north-west Indians. But as the knowledge of both

PREFACE. ix

may not only be useful, but necessary, I have given a comparative table of about two hundred and sixty words in both tongues, that the reader may use either as he shall find it best understood by the tribes with whom he may have occasion to trade ; though he will find, in a variety of instances, a perfect accordance.

The table of words in the Muhhekaneew, or Mohegan, and Shawanee tongues, are extracted from the Rev. Mr. Edwards's publication, and are inserted to shew their analogy with the Chippeway language ; and, as he observes that the language of the Delawares in Pennsylvania, of the Penobscots on the borders of Nova Scotia, of the Indians of St. Francis, in Canada, of the Shawanees on the Ohio, and many other tribes of Savages radically agree, I judged the tables of analogy would not be unacceptable.

In the course of the historical part, several speeches in the Chippeway language are introduced : and at the end of the Vocabulary, a number of familiar phrases, which not only serve to shew the mode of speech, but give a better idea of the language than single words.

The numeral *payshik*, or one, is frequently used to express the articles *a* and *the*; and *woke* is the general word for the plural number, though not always used.

Mr. Carver's Vocabulary will, in many instances, be found to differ from the Chippeway ; but when it is considered that though he calls it the Chippeway Vocabulary, in p. 414 of his work, he says " The Chippeway, or Algonkin," which evidently proves that he believes them the same language:—but with regard to the usefulness of the tongue, there is a perfect corroboration of sentiment; for he remarks that the Chippeway tongue appears to be the most prevailing of all the Indian languages.

It may not be amiss to observe, that the Chippeway tongue, as spoken by the servants of the Hudson's Bay Company, is somewhat different, though not essentially so, and is called by them the *Home-Guard* Language.

With regard to the Iroquois, or Mohawk tongue, which is peculiar to the Five and Six Nation Indians, it is not necessary in the fur trade beyond Michillimakinac; and if it were, there are not wanting printed authorities sufficient to instruct:—this consideration has induced me to give only the numerals, and a few words in the language.

I have not any thing further to add, but a sincere wish that my labours may prove useful to the world; and that whatever defects may be found in the following work, the Public will look on them with candour; and will recollect that they are perusing, not the pages of a professed *Tourist*, but such observations as a commercial man flatters himself may be found acceptable to the merchant and the philosopher.

ERRATA.

Page	Line			
29	21	*for* which	—	*read* And for which.
48	19	Pink-wood	—	—— Punk-wood.
50	3	at the entrance	—	—— near the entrance.
57	10	1800 weight	—	—— 18,000 weight.
76	14	Transaction	—	—— Transactions.
87	18	Nind	—	—— Nin
92	27	have not robbed me	—	—— have robbed me.
106	10	at the entrance	—	—— near the entrance.
108	10	Shunk	—	—— Skunk.
114	9	at Shunk's Lake	—	—— at the Skunk's Lake.
121	12	he desired	—	—— desired.
131	12	and entrusted	—	—— and to whom they entrusted.
149	25	Always	—	—— Also
179	2	Family	—	—— Families.

TO

SIR JOSEPH BANKS, BAR^T.

PRESIDENT

OF THE ROYAL SOCIETY, &c. &c. &c.

SIR,

I FEEL the highest satisfaction in being permitted to dedicate this work to one whose pursuits have ever been more peculiarly directed to objects of originality, and whose scientific researches have contributed so largely to the information and benefit of society.

The public are too well acquainted with your general knowledge in every branch of literature, to suspect that I hold the language of adulation. Should I attempt to do justice to a character so eminently distinguished, my feeble efforts could only be regarded as the grateful effusions of a

DEDICATION.

mind proud of a patronage that can ensure an especial share of public notice and protection.

I have the honour to be, very respectfully,

SIR,

Your most obedient servant,

London,
February, 1791.

J. LONG.

VOYAGES AND TRAVELS.

HAVING engaged myself, at an early period of life, to go to North America, in the quality of an articled clerk, I left Gravesend on the 10th of April, 1768, on board the Canada, captain Smith, bound to Quebec and Montreal. We had a pleasant voyage, till we reached the coast of America, when the weather proving unfavourable, we were obliged to put into Newfoundland, where we stayed fourteen days. Nothing remarkable occurred here, except that a party went on shore to hunt, and one of them, Mr. Jordan, who was a passenger, bound to Montreal, finding himself much fatigued, remained in the woods; the rest returned on board in the evening, anxiously expecting their companion; but after four days painful solicitude, not being able to obtain any intelligence of him, we gave up all hopes of seeing him again; and as the snow was deep on the ground, and the wild animals numerous, we supposed him to be either frozen to death, or devoured by the beasts. Just as the captain proposed setting sail, an Indian came on board, to whom we endeavoured to communicate our distress. On this occasion, he seemed to understand us, and made signs of his intention to go in search of him; and being furnished with some rum by way of encouragement, he got into his canoe and paddled ashore. The captain, with great humanity, deferred prosecuting the voyage for some time: but the Indian not returning, we left Newfoundland, and after a tedious passage of near eleven weeks, arrived at Quebec, the capital of Canada.

When the Spaniards (who first discovered this northern clime) sailed past Cape Rosiers at the entrance of the River St. Laurence, the mountains, now called the Mountains of Nôtre Dame, were covered with snow. Such a prospect, in the summer season, gave them a very unfavourable opinion of the country, and they were deterred from going up the river, supposing the land to be too barren to recompence their labours at present, or afford any future advantages; and the same impressions induced them to call it Capo di Nada, or Cape Nothing, by which name it is described in their charts, and from whence, by corruption of language, it has derived its present name of Canada.

The River St. Laurence takes it rise from Lake Nipissin, north-east of Lake Superior, about the distance of 2000 miles from Quebec. The breadth of it is 90 miles at the entrance, and it is navigable near 500 miles from the sea.

The Isle of Orleans, which is but a small distance from the city, is a beautiful spot of ground, about 20 miles in length, and six in breadth. The fertility of the soil makes it a useful and valuable garden, insomuch that it supplies the capital with vegetables and grain in great abundance. The opposite village of Beauport also charms the eye, and very much heightens the scene, which is rich, romantic, and magnificent.

The Fall of Montmorenci particularly attracted my notice, as it is perhaps the most pleasing natural cascade in the world; and though its height and width are not to be compared in point of awful grandeur with the stupendous cataract of Niagara, it is sufficiently wonderful to shew the power of the great Architect of the Universe; and its effects are more pleasing than the latter; for while it produces wonder and pleasure in the highest degree, it does not strike the beholder with such tremendous ideas.

As our ship was bound to Montreal, as well as Quebec, and I was under the captain's care and direction, he did not allow me to go on shore at the latter place; but in a few days, to my great joy, we arrived safe at Montreal, the place of our last destination.

Montreal, formerly called Ville Marie, has nothing remarkable in it at present; it was formerly famous for a great fair, which lasted near three months, and was resorted to by the Indians, who came from the distance of many hundreds of miles, to barter their peltry for English goods. It will give pleasure to the reader to be informed, that we received here the agreeable intelligence that Mr. Jordan was found in the woods, two days after our departure from Newfoundland, though with the loss of his feet, occasioned by the severity of the weather: he went afterwards in a vessel to Trois Riviéres, where he settled in an iron foundry.

Trois Riviéres, is so called from the junction of three currents which empty themselves into the River St. Laurence. About a league from the town there is an iron foundry, which was erected by private persons in the year 1737, and afterwards ceded to the King. At first cannon and mortars were cast there, but it is now principally used in the manufacture of stoves and kettles. The ore is taken at a small distance from the works. A river runs down from the foundry into the River St. Laurence, which enables the proprietors to send their manufactures round the country in boats upon very moderate terms.

This town, which is half way between Quebec and Montreal, had formerly a very considerable trade in peltry, and was the second mart in Canada; but in process of time the inhabitants of Montreal contrived to draw almost all the fur trade to themselves; and though the residents in Trois Riviéres live by their commerce with the savages, and the manufacturing of birch canoes, yet the town has lost that rank and consequence which it formerly maintained; nevertheless, the advantage of the iron foundry makes them some amends, and they live, upon the whole, as happy as any people in Canada. The inhabitants of Trois Riviéres were formerly very much incommoded with fleas, which swarmed in great quantities, and which, Baron de Lahontan humorously observes, occasioned an inconvenient quickness in conversation.

On my arrival at Montreal, I was placed under the care of a very respectable merchant to learn the Indian trade, which is the chief support of the town. I soon acquired the names of every article of commerce in the Iroquois and French languages, and being at once prepossessed in favour of the savages, improved daily in their tongue, to the satisfaction of my employer, who approving my assiduity, and wishing me to be completely qualified in the Mohawk language to enable me to traffic with the Indians in his absence, sent me to a village called

Cahnuaga, or Cocknawaga, situated about nine miles from Montreal, on the south side of the River St. Laurence, where I lived with a chief whose name was *Assenegetbter*, until I was sufficiently instructed in the language, and then returned to my master's store, to improve myself in French, which is not only universally spoken in Canada, but is absolutely necessary in the commercial intercourse with the natives, and without which it would be impossible to enjoy the society of the most respectable families, who are in general ignorant of the English language.

A Description of the Village and Inhabitants of Cahnuaga, *or* Cocknawaga, *who some years since separated from the* Mohawks.

The Savages of this nation, who are called the praying Indians, from the circumstance of their chiefs wearing crucifixes, and going through the streets of Montreal with their beads, begging alms, separated long since from the Mohawk and River Indians, and for a considerable time after their separation, carried on an illicit trade between Albany and Montreal. The village contains about two hundred houses, which, though they are chiefly built of stone, have a mean and dirty appearance. The inhabitants amount to about eight hundred, and (what is contrary to the general observation on the population of the Indians) are continually increasing. It is considered as the most respectable of all the Indian villages, and the people are in a great degree civilized and industrious. They sow corn, and do not depend like other nations solely upon hunting for support; but at the same time, they are not fond of laborious work, conceiving it only suited to those who are less free, and retaining so much of their primeval valour and independence as to annex the idea of slavery to every domestic employment. Their hunting grounds are within the United States, at a considerable distance from the village, round Fort George, Ticonderago, and Crown Point, where they kill beaver and deer, but not in such great abundance at present as they did formerly, the country being better inhabited, and the wild animals, from the present state of population, being obliged to seek a more distant and secure retreat. The skins they obtain are generally brought down to Montreal, and either sold for money, or bartered for goods. It is not improbable, that in a few years there will not be many good hunters among them, as they are extravagantly fond of dress, and that too of the most expensive kind. Their fondness for this luxury, which the profits arising from the lands they let out to the Canadians enables them to indulge, contributes to make them more idle; and in proportion as their vanity increases, ease and indolence are the more eagerly courted and gratified, insomuch that hunting is in danger of being totally abandoned. Their religion is Catholic, and they have a French priest, or, as the Chippeway Indians term it, "*The Master of Life's Man*," who instructs them, and performs divine service in the Iroquois tongue. Their devotion impressed my mind too powerfully to suffer it to pass unnoticed, and induces me to observe that great praise is due to their pastors, who by unwearied assiduity, and their own exemplary lives and conversation, have converted a savage race of beings from Heathenism to Christianity, and by uniformity of conduct, continue to preserve both their religion and themselves in the esteem of their converts: An example worthy of imitation, and amounting to an incontrovertible proof that nature, in her most degenerate state, may be reclaimed by those who are sincere in their endeavours, gentle in their manners, and consistent in the general tenor of their behaviour. And it is to be expected, and certainly most ardently to be wished, that the savage temper among them may in time be more effectually subdued, their natural impetuosity softened and restrained, and their minds weaned from their unhappy attachment to the use of strong liquors; their indulgence in which is frequently attended with the most melancholy and fatal consequences.

VOYAGES AND TRAVELS.

Of the INDIANS *of the Five and Six Nations.*

I shall now give a particular account of the Indians of the Five and Six Nations, and the reasons why they are so called, in order to enable the reader to form an idea of their consequence in a political point of view, as well as their importance on account of the fur trade; because the vicinity of the American territories from Georgia to New England, gives the United States a great command and influence from their situation, and renders them more to be dreaded than even the French were in the zenith of their American power, when it was universally known they had such an interest among the savages, as induced them to call the French their fathers, and of which so much yet remains, as to prompt them to retain a predilection in favour of the traders of the Gallic race who are settled among them.

In 1603, when the French settled in Canada, part of the Five Nations resided on the island of Montreal, and were at war with the Adirondacks (who lived on the Uttawa, or grand river leading to Michillimakinac); these, considered the Five Nations as very insignificant opponents, and incapable of serious revenge, and they were held in as much derision as the Delawares, who were usually called old women, or the Shawanees (who lived on the Wabach River), who were obliged to wear petticoats for a considerable time, in contempt of their want of courage, and as a badge of their pusillanimity and degradation. But as no people can bear the imputation of cowardice or effeminacy as a national character, the chiefs determined to rouse their young men, and stimulate them to retrieve, or establish, a reputation; and inspiring them with heroic notions, led them to war against the Satanas, or Shaounons, whom they subdued with great ease. This success revived their drooping spirits, and forgetting how often they had been defeated by the Adirondacks, commenced hostilities against them; and availing themselves of the mean opinion their enemies entertained of their valour, gained the victory in several actions: and at last carried on a successful war against them even in their own country, obliging their former conquerors to abandon their native land, and seek refuge on the spot where Quebec is now situated.

Soon after the French arrived and had settled at Quebec, they formed an alliance with the Adirondacks against the Five Nations. The first engagement proved decisive in favour of the Adirondacks, owing entirely to the use of fire arms having been introduced among them by their new allies, which the Indians of the Five Nations had never before seen. This alliance, and the consequent defeat was far from subduing or disheartening the Five Nations, but rather seemed to inspire them with additional ardour, and what they were deficient in military skill and suitable weapons, they supplied by stratagem and courage. Although the French gained several advantages over them in the course of more than fifteen years, they at length were glad to bring the contest to a conclusion, by making a peace with them.

This shews that the Savages of the Five Nations are not easily to be conquered, and proves the necessity of preserving them in our interest, as long as we shall deem it expedient, from policy, to keep possession of Canada. This being admitted, it is certain that no method will more effectually conduce to that end, than retaining such barriers in our hands as will enable us to afford them protection, and supply them with arms and ammunition, and other necessaries, in time of danger.

The Indians who lie to the north of Philadelphia, between the provinces of Pennsylvania and the Lakes, consist of three distinct leagues, of which the Senekas, Mohawks, and Onondagoes, who are called the fathers, compose the first; the Oneidoes, Cayugas, Tuscororas, Conoys and Nanticokes, which are one tribe, compose the second, and these two leagues constitute what is called the Six Nations. The third league is formed of the Wanamis, Chihokockis, or Delawares, the Mawhiccons, Munseys, and Wapingers, to which may be added the Mingoes. The Cowetas, or Creek Indians, are also united in friendship with them.

Mr. Colden says, the nations who are joined together by a league or confederacy, like the United Provinces of Holland, are known by the names of Mohawks, Oneydoes, Onondagoes, Cayugas, and Senekas; that each of these nations is again divided into three tribes or families, who are distinguished by the names of the Tortoise, Bear, and Wolf; and that the Tuscororas, after the war they had with the people of Carolina, fled to the Five Nations, and incorporated with them, so that in fact they now consist of six, although they still retain the name of the Five Nations. This union is of such long duration as to leave little or no traces of its origin.

Baron Lahontan observes, that the Iroquois are in reality but one nation, divided into five districts; and which he distinguishes in the following manner:— The Tsonontouans, the Goyogans, the Onontagues, the Oneyouts, and the Agnies, who were all settled about thirty leagues from each other, near the great Lake Frontenac, now called Ontario.

The Mohawks, or Maquas, are the most warlike among the Five Nations, and consist of near seven hundred warriors. They are called by the French, Agnies, or Annies, and were originally settled on the French or grand River, leading to Michillimakinac, from whence they afterwards removed to the Mohawk River, near Schenectady, about sixteen miles from Albany, in the state of New York. Since the war in 1757 they have separated, and part of the nation is settled on the grand river, near Niagara, and the rest at the back of the bay of Quenty, or Kenty, about forty-eight miles above Cataraqui, the capital of the Loyalist settlements on the River St. Laurence.

Cataraqui, or Fort Frontenac, is built near to the place where Lake Ontario discharges itself into the River St. Laurence. It was erected by Le Comte de Frontenac, governor general of Canada, to stop the incursions of the Iroquois, and divert the channel of the commerce in peltry, which that people carried on with the inhabitants of New York, and which they bartered for with the Savages by merchandize, at a cheaper rate than the French could supply them.

This fort was at first built of wood and turf, and surrounded with high pickets, but during the mission of Father Hennepin, it was faced with stone, by the direction of the Sieur Cavelier de la Salle, and enlarged to a circuit of more than seven hundred yards. The bason in which it stands is capable of holding a number of vessels of considerable burthen. There is a small garrison at present, and a commanding officer, to examine all boats which pass either to the new settlements or the upper posts.

The Oneidoes, or Oneyouts, the Onondagoes, Cayugas, Senekas, or Tsonontouans, and the Tuscororas, who live with the Oneidoes and Onondagoes, are settled about thirty leagues distant from each other, and none of them exceeding two hundred and fifty miles from the Mohawk River. All these nations express peace by the metaphor of a tree, whose top they say will reach the sun, and whose branches extend far abroad, not only that they may be seen at a great distance, but to afford them shelter and repose.

The Five Nations claim all the country south of the River St. Laurence to the Ohio, and down the Ohio to the Wabache, which lies to the westward of the state of Pennsylvania, near to the borders of Virginia; westerly, to the Lakes Ontario and Erie, and the River Miamis, and the eastern boundaries of Lake Champlain, and the United States.

The firmness of this league, the great extent of land it claims, the number of great warriors it produces, and the undaunted courage and skill which distinguish the members of it in their contests both with the Savages and European nations, all conspire to prove the good policy of an alliance with them; as it is an undoubted fact, that in case of a dispute with the Americans, the posts would make but a feeble resist-

VOYAGES AND TRAVELS.   13

ance without their exertions; and deprived of the forts, the fur trade would soon be lost to this country.

I shall next consider the situation and utility of these barriers, in a commercial point of view, and endeavour to shew the propriety of keeping possession of the posts, notwithstanding by the treaty of peace with the United States, they were expressly stipulated to be given up; although it is not probable indeed that the Americans will be able to fulfil the treaty on their part, so as to entitle them to make a reasonable demand—I mean such a claim as government must absolutely admit.

The first post I shall notice is Oswegatche, on the River St. Laurence, about one hundred and fifty miles above Montreal, at the mouth of the Black River, where there are about an hundred Savages, who occasionally frequent it, and are called Oswegatche Indians, although they belong to the tribes of the Five Nations. To this fort the inhabitants of New England may with ease transport goods, to supply the Mohawks, Cahnuagas, Connecedagas, St. Regis, and some straggling Messesawger Indians, who live near the Détroit, at a smaller expence than they can possibly be obtained from the merchants at Quebec or Montreal, but particularly Rum, which is now become an essential requisite in every transaction with the Savages; for though they used formerly often to complain of the introduction of strong water by the traders (as appears by the language of their chiefs in council) to the prejudice of their young men, yet they have not now the resolution to refrain from the use of it;—on the contrary, it is become so familiar, and even necessary to them, that a drunken frolic is looked upon as an indispensible requisite in a barter, and anticipated with extreme delight.

Carlton Island is higher up the river, and has greater conveniences annexed to it than Oswegatche, having an excellent harbour, with a strong fortification well garrisoned. It affords excellent accommodation for shipping, and may be considered as the naval storehouse for supplying Niagara and the other posts. There are vessels of considerable bulk continually sailing from thence to Niagara, Oswego, &c.— There is also a commodore of the Lakes, whose residence is on the island.

Fort Oswego, on Lake Ontario, formerly called Lake Frontenac, is a good fortification, and capable of containing six hundred men. This post is particularly important, as it is the key to the United States, and commands the opening to the North, or Hudson's River, protecting the trade with the Indians who live on the banks of the River St. Laurence, and the whole extent of the great sheet of water near which it stands, reckoned about eighty leagues in length, and in some places from twenty-five to thirty broad.

When the English were in possession of the Colonies, Albany commanded the trade with the Indians; and it is well known that no place in America furnished such a quantity of furs and skins, not even the Hudson's Bay settlements, whose utmost extent of trade is far inferior to the produce collected here. These furs and skins were procured from Canada, and brought to Fort Oswego by the Indians, who disposed of them to the agents sent there by the merchants of Albany.

Besides, Indian goods may be conveyed from Albany to Fort Oswego at a cheaper rate than from Montreal to the new settlements at Cataraqui and the head of the Bay of Kenty, and at less risk, because the stream of the Mohawk River is not so strong as that of the Cataraqui River, between the Lake and Montreal, and there are not so many falls of water.

Fort Niagara is on the same lake, where there is also a good garrison. This lake takes its rise from Lake Erie, and after a course of fifteen leagues, empties itself into Lake Ontario. About four leagues before it enters the lake, it is intercepted by the great fall which is mentioned by various authors, who do not agree in opinion respecting its height; but from the most authentic accounts, joined to my own observations, I am inclined to coincide with the judgment of captain Pieric, who made an actual survey, and describes the height to be one hundred and forty-six feet, and the width one thousand and forty, which proves that the accounts of Father Hennepin and La Salle were erroneous, who both agree in calling the perpendicular height six hundred feet. The distance from Fort Niagara to Fort Stanwix is about two hundred and eighty miles, through the Jenesee country, which I travelled with great ease in about eight days. This post therefore is of the most essential importance to protect the Indians who are in alliance with Great Britain, and to secure the valuable and undivided advantage of their trade.

The Détroit is so called from being a strait between Lake Erie, and Lake Huron, and commands the trade from the Ohio, Illinois, Mississippi, and the Upper Lakes, which post is resorted to by the Uttawas,

Hurons, Miamis, Ohio, Mississippi, Delaware, and Tuscorora Indians, besides the Messesawgas.

These five posts are situated at the back of the three states of New England, New York, and Pennsylvania, and at a very small distance from the Loyalist settlements.

The last post is Michillimakinac, which is situated between Lake Huron and Lake Michigan, upon an isthmus, about one hundred and thirty leagues long, and twenty-two wide, and is the last fortress towards the north-west. This point of land is on the north of the straits through which the Lake of the Hinois, or Michigan, three hundred leagues in circumference, empties itself into Lake Huron, which is of equal extent. The strait is about three leagues long, and one broad, and half a league distant from the mouth of the Hinois.

This is perhaps the most material of all the barriers, and of the greatest importance to the commercial interest of this country, as it intercepts all the trade of the Indians of the upper country from Hudson's Bay to Lake Superior, and affords protection to various tribes of Savages, who constantly resort to it to receive presents from the commanding officer, and from whence the traders, who go to the north-west, take their departure for the grand portage, or grand carrying place, which is nine miles in length, before they enter on the waters communicating with the north-west.

Were the English to remain in possession of every part of Canada, except the posts, numberless doors would be left open for the Americans to smuggle in their goods, and in process of time the illicit trade would supersede the necessity of the exportation of British goods from England to Canada, and the commercial benefits arising from the consumption of our manufactures would be entirely lost.—In that case, Canada would be of little service to England in a commercial point of view: How far it is worth the expence of retaining, politically considered, is not for me to discuss.

18   VOYAGES AND TRAVELS.

Indian Scouts, and Manner of Scalping.

HAVING endeavoured to explain the nature and importance of the Five and Six Nation Indians, and described the situation of the posts, and the probable consequences of complying with the treaty, I shall return to my situation at Montreal.

Having stayed with my employer seven years, and not being willing to enter into a new agreement, I determined to pursue the bent of my inclinations; and being naturally of a roving disposition, which was increased by my frequent associations with the Savages, I entered a volunteer at the head of a party of Indians, thinking that my country might at some future period derive advantage from my more intimate knowledge of the country and its language.

My *entrée* was in 1775, when a party of about thirty of the Americans, commanded by the famous Ethan Allen, appeared at Long Point, about two miles from Montreal, intending to plunder the town; they were however disappointed in their expectations by the good conduct of captain Crawford of the twenty-sixth regiment, who with about forty regulars and some volunteers sallied out and made the enemy retreat to a barn, where an engagement took place, in which major Carden, Mr. Paterson, a volunteer, and three privates were killed, and I was wounded in the foot; but on the arrival of a field piece, the enemy surrendered.

VOYAGES AND TRAVELS. 19

Being beloved by the Indians, and preferring active service with them to any other mode of life, I accompanied lieutenant Peter Johnson and lieutenant Walter Butler, with a few Mohawks, to attack the Americans at Isle au Noix, whom we defeated, taking a great many prisoners. During the engagement we lost two volunteers and three privates. In this action I received a wound in the head from the butt-end of a musket.

I then joined the eighth regiment of foot, commanded by captain Foster, to attack the Americans at the Cedars, whom we also defeated. The prisoners were left at Fort St. Vielle, or Prison Island, at the foot of the Falls, under a proper guard; and the remains of our small army, consisting of about one hundred and fifty men, went down to La Chine to engage another body of Americans; but finding them too strongly entrenched, we retreated to Point Clair, where we stayed till we received intelligence that general Arnold, with four thousand men were at Isle au Noix, and that major Gordon was killed in his way to St. John's, about two miles from the fort. On this occasion it may not be amiss to observe, that the custom adopted by the Americans, and with so much success, of levelling their pieces at the officers, originated with the Indians, who are possessed with an idea that the men will naturally be thrown into confusion when their leaders are dead. This however is not without exceptions: the Mattaugwessawacks, whose country lies westward of Lake Superior, hold the persons of officers sacred; and Josepsis, one of their tribe, who was taken prisoner, and sold to the Penobscot Indians, says that the Savages they were at war with have adopted the same method.

D 2

I was immediately ordered on a scout, at the head of ten Conneccdaga or Rondaxe Indians, with captain La Motte, a Canadian gentleman, in search of the person who had killed major Gordon, and to reconnoitre the woods, in hopes of gaining information of the real force of the Americans at Isle au Noix. To avoid suspicion, we were all dressed like Savages; and as captain La Motte and myself were well acquainted with the Iroquois language, it was impossible to distinguish us from the natives. We were out six days and nights, with very little provision, living chiefly on the scrapings of the inner bark of trees and wild roots, particularly onions, which grow in great abundance, and are not disagreeable to the palate. Hunger reconciles us to every thing that will support nature, and makes the most indifferent food acceptable. From my own woful experience I can assert, that what at any other time would have been unpleasant and even nauseous, under the pressure of hunger is not only greedily eaten, but relished as a luxury. Those who are acquainted with the nature of roving in the woods in time of war, know the necessity of travelling light, and particularly on an Indian scout, as the Savages seldom take any thing but a small quantity of Indian corn and Maple sugar, which, after beating the corn between two stones, they mix with water, and on this they subsist. During this expedition, as the business was urgent, and the enemy near at hand, we depended on adventitious food.

On the last day's march, returning without being able to obtain any intelligence, one of the Indians heard a noise resembling the breaking of a stick; the chief of the band sent out a scout, who soon returned with a prisoner. The man appeared much frightened, imagining himself in the hands of Savages only. Having bound him to a tree, I being the only one of the party who understood English, questioned him very closely respecting the situation and force of the enemy, and interpreted the conversation. When he heard me talk his own language he was agreeably surprised, and his fears in some degree giving way to hope, he begged me to save him from the fury of the Indians, whose general conduct in war had filled his mind with the most dreadful apprehensions. I assured him, that if he would faithfully satisfy all my inquiries, his life should be spared. He cheerfully complied with the requisition, and directed me to a place from whence we might have a clear view of the Americans, who were encamped on the opposite shore.

Having left him bound, we proceeded about two miles through swamps, till we came in sight of the enemy. The Indians immediately panted for action, but captain La Motte thought it prudent to restrain their ardour, and ordered them to retreat into the woods, still keeping our object in view. Soon after, a boat full of men crossed the river, and landed without perceiving us. The Indians instantly kindled a fire, and each man filled his blanket with rotten wood and leaves, till it was extended to the size of a man; then placing them near the fire, to appear like Indians asleep, they retired to a small distance, to give the Americans an opportunity of coming up unmolested, not doubting but they would immediately fire at the blankets. The manœuvre succeeded to our expectation; for the Americans discovering the smoke advanced towards the fire, and perceiving the blankets, discharged their muskets. The Savages immediately rushed from their ambush, and setting up the war-hoop, fell upon the enemy, scalped seven of them, and took five prisoners, whom we painted like ourselves. We then returned, released the prisoner from the tree, and conducted them all to St. John's, where they were examined by colonel England, who ordered me to take them to Sir Guy Carleton without delay.

Having executed this commission to the satisfaction of the commander in chief, I remained some time with my old friends, till I received a message from Sir Guy Carleton to attend him; when he ordered me to join brigadier general Nesbit, with the twenty-ninth and forty-seventh regiments; in the latter of which I served as a volunteer a considerable time; but finding no vacancy, and having no allowance for my services, to enable me to live and appear as I wished, I quitted the regiment to enjoy my favourite Indian life; and as I knew their manner of living, and could accommodate myself to their diet, I thought I might probably continue serviceable to my country in scouting parties, and accordingly accompanied a party of Savages to the Lake of the two Mountains, fifteen leagues above Montreal, a village belonging to the Connecedagas, carrying a scalp as a trophy of my services.

Scalping is a mode of torture peculiar to the Indians. If a blow is given with the tomahawk previous to the scalp being taken off, it is followed by instant death; but where scalping only is inflicted, it puts the person to excruciating pain, though death does not always ensue. There are instances of persons of both sexes, now living in America, and no doubt in other countries, who, after having been scalped, by wearing a plate of silver or tin on the crown of the head, to keep it from cold, enjoy a good state of health, and are seldom afflicted with pains.

When an Indian strikes a person on the temple with a tomahawk, the victim instantly drops; he then seizes his hair with one hand, twisting it very tight together, to separate the skin from the head, and placing his knee on the breast, with the other he draws the scalping knife from the sheath, and cuts the skin round the forehead, pulling it off with his teeth. As he is very dexterous, the operation is generally performed in two minutes. The scalp is then extended on three hoops, dried in the sun, and rubbed over with vermilion. Some of the Indians in time of war, <u>when scalps are well paid for</u>, divide one into five or six parts, and carry them to the nearest post, in hopes of receiving a reward proportionate to the number.

When the scalp is taken from the head of one of their own people, they frequently make the dead body of advantage to them, by dressing it up and painting it with vermilion; they then place it against a tree, with weapons in its hand, to induce the Indians to suppose it an enemy on the watch; and <u>round the body they set spears in the ground</u>, so as scarcely to be discernible. The Indians, on seeing the person against the tree, and anxious to make him a prisoner, in the eagerness of running fall on the points of the spears, and being disabled from proceeding, are easily made prisoners.

Before I close this subject I shall relate an anecdote of two Savages of different nations, in the time of Sir William Johnson.

A Mohawk, of the name of Scunnionsa, or the elk, and a Chippeway Indian of the name of Cark Cark, or the crow, having met at a council of war near Crown Point, in the year 1757, were extolling their own merits, and boasting of their superiority in taking scalps. The Mohawk contended that he could take a larger scalp than the Chippeway war-

24   VOYAGES AND TRAVELS.

rior; who was very highly offended, and desired that the experiment might be made. They parted, each pursuing a different route, after having first agreed to meet at a certain place, on a particular day, when a council was to be held. At the time appointed they returned, and appeared at the council. The Mohawk laid down his scalp, which was the skin of the head and neck of a man stuffed with fine moss, and sewed up with deers' sinews, and the eyes fastened in. The chiefs expressed their approbation, and pronounced him to be a great and brave warrior. The Chippeway then rose, and looking earnestly at the Mohawk, desired the interpreter to tell him that it was an old woman's scalp, which is considered as a term of great reproach, and called to one of his sons to bring forward his scalp; when instantly he exhibited to their view the complete skin of a man, stuffed with down feathers, and sewed very close with deers' sinews. The chiefs loaded him with praise, and unanimously acknowledged his superiority. The Mohawk warrior, fired with resentment, withdrew from the council meditating revenge; and as soon as he saw the Chippeway come forth, he followed him, and watching a convenient opportunity, dispatched him with his tomahawk, rejoicing that he had, even in this dastardly manner, got rid of a victorious rival.

> *[Marginalia:]* These Murderers in our pay, and presiding make a right of blood actions in our very presence — surely England will pay one day for this?
>
> The Murderers our beloved ally.

Some Account of the Character and Disposition of the CONNECEDAGA, *or* RONDAXE INDIANS; *with Remarks on the* IROQUOIS *and* CHEROKEE *Nations.*

THE Savages of this nation are of the Chippeway tribe, and speak a mixture of the Iroquois and Chippeway tongues: they were driven from the upper country at the time of the great Indian war, about the year 1720, and settled on the Lake of the two Mountains. There are about two hundred inhabitants, who are very industrious, and cultivate the land in the manner of the Cahnuagas; they also breed cattle, and live in a degree of civilization unknown to most of the Chippeway tribes. There is also a town near Lake Erie, in the limits of the United States, which is inhabited by about fifteen hundred of this nation, of whom the Reverend Mr. Charles Beattie gives a very favourable account.

Since the settlement of the Connecedagas they have intermarried with the Cahnuaga, St. Regis, and Mohawk Indians, which is the reason why their language is less pure, though some of them speak the original tongue, which in my frequent communications with the Chippeways beyond Michillimakinac, I found in every respect perfectly understood. It was among these Indians that I first acquired the rudiments of a language which, from long habit, is become more familiar to me than my own; and I hope I shall not be accused of vanity, in asserting that the vocabulary and familiar phrases, subjoined to this work, are more copious than will be found in any former publication. In spelling them I have been particularly careful in using such letters and accents as best express the Indian words, according to our pronunciation. To lay down general rules for the orthography of a language which has never been reduced to a system, I do not pretend: my endeavours may perhaps assist those who are better informed in the principles of universal grammar.

The Connecedagas are esteemed brave warriors; and my opinion, founded on long experience of their conduct and bravery, coincides with that which the English, from report only, entertain of them. No nation of Savages were ever more true to the British interest, not even the Mohawks, whose fidelity is become almost proverbial. During the continuance of the American war, they neglected their families and domestic concerns to fight for the English, which the Cahnuagas (though descendants of the Mohawks and Munseys, or Mawhiccon Indians, commonly called River Indians) did not with so much cheerfulness; perhaps the relationship of the latter to the Delawares before their defection, whom the Indians by way of derision used to call old women, might occasion this temporary reluctance; but if that was the cause, it was but of very short duration; for to do them justice, when they took up the tomahawk they behaved with great intrepidity, and proved that the blood of the ancient Mohawks still ran in their veins. Some have, though I think without much candour, imputed their services to the fear of our government, and the resentment of the Savages in our interest on the one hand, and the hopes of considerable rewards on the other; but as such reflections may be far from the truth, it cannot answer any purpose to comment severely on their con-

> *Sic* virtuous Scalpers even neglect their families for us.— What fine fellows for a limited Monarchy to connect with."

duct: it is sufficient to know they were our allies, and in all probability will continue friendly to the British nation. Great praise is due on this account to major Carlton, a brave and experienced officer, whom they loved with a Roman friendship; they flew to his standard with alacrity, obeyed him with cheerfulness, and never deserted him: no instance of friendship or attachment, either ancient or modern, could surpass it.

It requires good natural sense, and a thorough knowledge of the dispositions of the Indians, to persuade them to place unlimited confidence in their European or American leaders; to which must always be added, a seeming approbation of their advice, and an endeavour to conform to their wishes, never obstinately pursuing a design either offensive or defensive, contrary to their opinion. How fatal a different line of conduct may prove, the destruction of general Braddock is a melancholy instance: by his haughty demeanour, and strict adherence to his own plan, in direct opposition to the counsel of experienced chiefs, he lost their friendship, and died unlamented, confirming them in an opinion they had before often hinted, " that he wanted both skill " and prudence in war." Even the great Washington incurred their censure by his conduct, and gave occasion to an Indian chief, of the name of Thanachrishon, of the Seneka tribes, judging him by their own rules, to say, " that he was a good natured man, but had no ex- "perience."

An impartial mind will require but little to be persuaded that the Indians are superior to us in the woods: it is their natural element (if I may be allowed the expression), and a tree or river, of which their recollection never fails, guide them to the secret recesses of a deep wood, either for safety, or the purpose of ambush. As they pay little attention to the rising or setting sun, it at first surprised me, by what method they travel from place to place, without any material aberration; but this they soon explained, by assuring me, that they had not the least difficulty in going from one spot to another, being governed by the moss on the trees, which always remains on the north side, but on the south it wastes and decays: they remark also, that the branches are larger, and the leaves more luxuriant on the south than on the north side of the tree. The most enlightened part of mankind, I am persuaded, cannot be more exact in their mode of judging, nor more attentive to the works of nature.

To prove further, if there are any who doubt it, that the Indians possess strong natural abilities, and are even capable of receiving improvement from the pursuits of learning, I shall relate a story from Kalm's Travels.

" An old American Savage being at an inn at New York, met with a gentleman who gave him some liquor, and being rather lively, boasted he could read and write English. The gentleman, willing to indulge him in displaying his knowledge, begged leave to propose a question, to which the old man consented. He was then asked, who was the first circumcised? the Indian immediately replied, father Abraham:—and directly asked the gentleman, who was the first quaker? He said it was very uncertain; that people differed in their sentiments exceedingly. The Indian perceiving the gentleman unable to resolve the question, put his fingers into his mouth, to express his surprize, and looking stedfastly, told him, that Mordecai was the first quaker, for he would not pull off his hat to Haman."

Mr. Adair says, the Cherokees are very apt at giving people nicknames. A dull stalking fellow, they call a turkey buzzard; an ill tempered man, a wasp; a talkative person, a grasshopper; a hoarse voice, they say resembles a bull; and an interpreter whose manners and conversation are obscene, they call a smock interpreter.

The disposition of the Indians is naturally proud and self-sufficient: they think themselves the wisest of the sons of men, and are extremely offended when their advice is rejected. The feats of valour of their ancestors, continually repeated and impressed upon their minds, inspire them with the most exalted notions of their own prowess and bravery; hence arises the firmest reliance on their own courage and power; and though but a handful of men, comparatively speaking, they are vain enough to think they can overthrow both French and English whenever they please. They say, the latter are fools, for they hold their guns half man high, and let them snap; but that they themselves take sight, and seldom fail of doing execution, which, they add, is the true intention of going to war.

These exalted notions of self-consequence are more peculiar to the Five Nations, for which they are more eminently distinguished than other tribes of Savages, although none of them are deficient in this respect. Such sentiments as these have made the Iroquois dreaded and revered by others, for their superior understanding and valour, and likewise has a tendency to increase their fame. Although they decrease in numbers daily, the thirst of glory will never be extinguished among them, whilst there is a breast to nourish it: they will never shrink from danger when honour is at stake.

The Iroquois laugh when you talk to them of obedience to kings; for they cannot reconcile the idea of submission with the dignity of man. Each individual is a sovereign in his own mind; and as he conceives he derives his freedom from the great Spirit alone, he cannot be induced to acknowledge any other power.

They are extremely jealous, and easily offended, and when they have been once induced to suspect, it is very difficult to remove the impression. They carry their resentments with them to the grave, and bequeath them to the rising generation.

Those who have associated with them, though they may admire their heroism in war, their resolution in supporting the most excruciating tortures, and the stability of their friendships, cannot but lament the dreadful effects of their displeasure, which has no bounds. It is this violence of temper, which is generally in the extreme, that makes them so difficult to subdue, and so dangerous to encourage; too much indulgence they attribute to fear, and too much severity brings on resentment.

To remove these strong prejudices (which, however prone human nature may be to encourage them, would never prove so prejudicial to society, unless continually promoted by the advice and example of the aged), has been the constant endeavour of those nations who have been in alliance with them, and some attempts have been made to soften their manners by the introduction of the Christian religion, whose precepts are so wonderfully calculated to destroy every blood-thirsty sentiment, and make mankind happier in themselves, and better members of the community. In this laudable pursuit our neighbours the French have been most successful, at least so far as an alteration in external behaviour may be considered as an indication of the amendment of the heart. The good conduct of the inhabitants of several Indian villages in Canada bears testimony to this observation. Nevertheless, in contradiction to this remark, Mr. James Adair observes, that the French Canadians are highly censurable for debauching our peaceble Northern Indians with their " infernal catechism."

[marginalia: And then we go a Scalping with them! against Christians.]

Though I am not an advocate for creeds inimical to the peace of society, I believe the censure is too severe, for however formerly they might have been influenced by bigotted priests instilling into their minds sentiments unfavourable to the subjects of Great Britain, I am clearly of opinion, that they have for many years used their best endeavours to inculcate the principles of the Gospel; indeed, it is always to be lamented when either politics or religion are made subservient to each other: this being properly considered, perhaps the French are not more blameable than other nations. We are too apt to involve others in our disputes, and religion is too frequently introduced by bigots to assist the cause they wish to support.

With regard to those Indians who have been accustomed to the society of English traders, and even preachers (sorry am I to observe it), their sentiments, manners, and practices are very different. The

[marginalia: If this picture is true, ought we not to blush whenever we use the word Savage again, which with so much propriety may be applied to our regular government.]

alteration is manifestly for the worse; they have become more degenerate, and added to the turbulence of passions unsubdued by reason the vices of lying and swearing, which unfortunately they have learned from us.

The testimony of Mr. Sargeant, a gentleman of New England, supports this assertion; who relates, that in a journey to the Shawanese Indians (the allies and dependants of the Six Nations), and some other tribes, when he offered to instruct them in the Christian religion, they rejected it with disdain; they even reproached Christianity, told him the traders would lie, cheat, and debauch their young women, and even their wives, when the husbands were from home. They further added, that the Senekas had given them their country, but charged them never to receive Christianity from the English.

I shall subjoin one more proof to this. Governor Hunter, by order of Queen Anne, presented the Indians with cloaths, and other things of which they were extremely fond; and addressing them at a council, which was held at Albany, told them that their good mother the Queen had not only generously provided them with fine cloaths for their bodies, but likewise intended to adorn their souls by the preaching of the Gospel, and that some ministers should be sent to instruct them. When the governor had finished his speech, the oldest chief rose up and said, that, in the name of all the Indians, he thanked their good mother the Queen for the fine cloaths she had sent them; but that in regard to the ministers, they had already some of them, who, instead of preaching the Gospel to them, taught them to drink to excess, to cheat and quarrel among themselves, and entreated the governor to take from them the preachers, and a number of Europeans who came among them; for before their arrival, the Indians were honest, sober and innocent people; but now most of them were rogues; that they <u>formerly had the fear of God</u>: but that <u>now they hardly believed his existence</u>.

[margin note: mark the keeping of a connection with corrupted nation.]

To extenuate as much as possible this charge against the English, let it be observed, that the vice and immorality complained of, is to be attributed in a great measure to the traders, <u>who used to purchase convicts</u>, and hire men of infamous character to carry up their goods among the Indians, many of whom ran away from their masters to join the Savages: the iniquitous conduct of those people essentially injured the English in the opinion of the Indians, and fixed an odium which will not be soon or easily removed.

[margin note: This is a very poor extenuation, and only proves that they made slaves of men of our own colour, country, and religious faith.]

Description of the INDIAN Dances,- &c.

HAVING finished this long digression, I shall continue my history from the time of going to the village of the Connecedagas, where I stayed some months, making several excursions in scouting parties, and frequently bringing in prisoners, which did not escape the notice of Sir Guy Carleton, who at the next interview approved my conduct, and wished me to serve again in his regiment. I told him I was extremely happy I had rendered myself useful to my country, and considered myself highly honoured by so flattering a mark of his approbation; but that the life of a volunteer, though very honourable, would not entitle me to pay, and there was not a vacancy in any of the British regiments: he then appointed me a midshipman on board the ship Fell, commanded by captain Barnsfer, lying in the river St. Laurence, in which service I continued till she was ordered for England.

As soon as I quitted the navy, I returned to the Lake of the Two Mountains, and continued doing my utmost, in the line of an interpreter, and at intervals perfecting myself in the Indian languages, particularly in the Chippeway tongue, as I purposed engaging in the service of a merchant, to go to the north west the first convenient opportunity. I also applied myself sedulously to obtain a complete knowledge of their manners and customs, and with that view partook of their amusements, and was soon noticed as a good dancer. To this qualification I also added the perfect notes of the different war hoops, as naturally as a Savage; and by conforming to their ways, and taking pleasure in their diversions, I was soon endeared to them, and left them with regret.

The dances among the Indians are many and various, and to each of them there is a particular hoop.

1. The calumet dance.
2. The war dance.
3. The chiefs' dance.
4. The set out dance.
5. The scalp dance.
6. The dead dance.
7. The prisoner's dance.
8. The return dance.
9. The spear dance.
10. The marriage dance.
11. The sacrifice dance.

All these I was perfect master of, frequently leading the sett. If accidentally a stranger came among us, (unless I chose to be noticed) no one could distinguish me from the Indians.

Presuming on my appearing exactly like a Savage, I occasionally went down in a canoe to Montreal, and frequently passed the posts as an Indian. Sometimes I would distinguish myself at a charivari, which is a custom that prevails in different parts of Canada, of assembling with old pots, kettles, &c. and beating them at the doors of new married people; but generally, either when the man is older than the woman, or the parties have been twice married: in those cases they beat a charivari, hallooing out very vociferously, until the man is obliged to obtain their silence by pecuniary contribution, or submit to be abused with the vilest language. Charivari, in French, means a paltry kind of music, which I suppose is the origin of the custom.

Not content with being a proficient in their sports, I learnt to make a canoe, bark a tree for the purpose, and perform the whole business as regular as the natives. I also made makissins, or Indian shoes, of dear skins, drest and smoked to make the leather soft and pliable, and worked with porcupine quills and small beads, to which are sometimes suspended hawk bells. Those made by the Mohawks, at the Grand River near Niagara, are preferred for their superior workmanship and taste, and are sometimes sold so high as four dollars a pair, but in general they may be purchased, without ornaments, for one dollar: they are more pleasant to wear than English shoes: in summer they are cooler to the feet, and in winter, from being made roomy, they will admit a thick sock, to prevent the excessive cold from penetrating. The Indians, in their war dances, sew hawk bells and small pieces of tin on them to make a jingling noise, and at a dance where I was present, these, with the addition of a large horse bell, which I gave the chief who led the dance, made a noise not much unlike a Dutch concert.

The Savages are esteemed very active and nimble footed, but admitting this general opinion to prevail, it is well known the Europeans are more swift in running a small distance: their chief merit, I am of opinion, consists in their being able to continue a long time in one steady pace, which makes them useful in going express through the woods; and as they require little sleep, and can subsist on roots and water, which they take *en volant*, they do not waste much time in refreshment. They are also admirable swimmers, and are not afraid of the strongest current. With these qualifications they are certainly a very useful race of men; and as long as the English retain any possessions in Canada, should be considered as the most valuable acquisition; indeed, as indispensibly necessary; and every endeavour should be exerted to retain them in our interest.

With regard to bodily strength, they are excelled by many; and even in hunting, the Virginians equal them in every part of the chace, though all the world allow them the merit of being good marksmen. I remember seeing some Americans shooting at a loon, a bird nearly the size of an English goose. This bird is remarkable for diving, and generally rises some yards from the place where it dips. They fired at the distance of one hundred and fifty yards with a rifle, several times without success: an Indian standing by, laughed at them, and told them they were old women; they desired him to try his skill, which he instantly did: taking his gun, and resting it against a tree, he fired, and shot the loon through the neck. I confess I never saw a better shot in my life, and was highly pleased, as it gratified my pride, in giving the Americans a favourable opinion of the Savages, for whom I always entertained a predilection.

The loon is a very remarkable bird, from the formation of its feet: but having no anatomical knowledge, I cannot describe it technically. They are so made, that it can scarcely walk; it is therefore seldom seen on land. In calm weather it rises from the water with great difficulty, and flies as impelled by the wind, on which it seems to depend. The method usually adopted by the Indians to kill these birds, is by fixing a large bough at the head of the canoe, to conceal themselves till they paddle near the place where they are; when at a convenient distance, they fire, though not always with success. In the Chippeway language it is called a maunk, which agrees with the French word manquer, to fail; it being, from its shyness, very difficult to kill. The skin, which is very tough and thick, is dried and made use of as cases to cover their guns, to prevent the wet from spoiling them.

Having grown tired of living entirely with the Savages, I made an excursion to Montreal, where I met with an offer to go as interpreter to the north, which, at first, I did not care to accept; but as the salary proposed was handsome, upon mature deliberation, I embraced the opportunity of entering into that way of life, from which I fully expected profit at least, if not pleasure; but alas! I had often abundant reason to repent the pursuing the bent of my inclinations.

On the fourth of May, 1777, I left Montreal, with two large birch canoes, called by the French, maître canots, having ten Canadians in each, as the number of portages require many hands to transport the goods across the landings, which can only be done on men's shoulders. As their voyage is so essentially different from the English manner of travelling, I shall relate it particularly.

The canoes are made at Trois Riviéres; they are, in general, eight fathoms long, and one and a half wide, covered with the bark of the birch tree, and sewed very close with fibrous roots; and of this size they will carry four tons weight each. As early in the spring as the ice will permit, they are brought up to La Chine, a village nine miles above Montreal.

La Chine takes its name from the following story. Le Sieur La Salle, who was afterwards murdered by two of his own party, in Canada, in the year 1686, was very intent on discovering a shorter road to China than was then known, but his project failing by an accident which happened to him at this place, he was obliged to postpone his journey to the east, which induced the Canadians, by way of derision, to call it La Chine, or China; and by that name it has ever since been known.

At this place the Indian goods are put on board very carefully; the dry merchandise in bales about eighty pounds weight, the rum, powder, and shot, in small kegs. The voyage from Trois Riviéres to La Chine is tedious and troublesome, as there is a strong current to combat; and without a fair wind, and occasionally a brisk gale to assist or relieve the constant use of the paddles, it would be impossible to make any way. Where the water is shallow, the canoes must be forced forward with long setting poles, while the men wade knee-deep, and pull against the current with ropes; this is a labour and fatigue beyond what will be easily imagined. Custom has however made the Canadians very expert, and I must do them the justice to say they encounter these difficulties with uncommon chearfulness, though they sometimes exclaim, " C'est la misere, mon bourgeois."

From La Chine to Michillimakinac, there are thirty six portages; the distance by land and water is about nine hundred miles : in favourable weather the journey is frequently performed in about a month. Great care is necessary to steer the canoes up the strong rapids; to labour and care must also be added experience to keep them upright, and prevent their striking or rubbing against the stones, as they are very slight, and easily damaged. Whenever by accident they receive an injury, as they frequently do, the hole is stopped with gum, melted with a piece of charcoal; the gum by wetting immediately becomes hard, and is capable of resisting the impression of the water. When the hole is too large to be stopped by gum only, the inner bark of the birch tree, pounded and tempered like mortar, is put on the aperture, this is covered by a linen rag, and the edges firmly cemented with gum.

We continued our voyage to La Barriére, at the head of the Long Saut, or long water fall, a very dangerous current from the extreme rapidity of the fall. At the top of this fall there are some traders settled, but they are not of any consequence either for the extent of their commerce, or the profits arising from the peltry they collect, the Savages in those parts being too well acquainted with the value of furs and skins to be imposed upon, unless when they are intoxicated, an advantage I must confess too frequently taken.

From this fall we proceeded to the Lake of the two Mountains, where there is a village belonging to the Connecedaga Indians, already described. At this place I stayed a day among my old friends, which was all the time my engagements would allow, as it is of the most material consequence in this branch of trade to be early at the wintering ground.

We proceeded to the Uttawa, or Grand River, coasting all the way till we came to Lake Nipissin, from whence the River St. Laurence takes its rise. We then entered the French River, leading to Lake Huron, and proceeded with very favourable weather to Michillimakinac, where we arrived on the 17th of June.

The country every where abounds with wild animals, particularly bears, moose and other deer, beavers, beaver eaters, lynx, foxes, squirrels, fishers, otters, martins, minx, wood cats, racoons, wolves, musquashes, &c.——There are scarce any but savage inhabitants to be found, who rove from place to place for subsistance, feeding on the animals they kill, except the skunk, or pole cat, which they never eat, unless pressed by the most extreme hunger.

Monsieur La Salle relates, that in his voyage on the banks of the Mississippi, among the nation of the Oumas, who live on a river of the same name, he saw a most extraordinary animal between the wolf and the lion; the head and shape resembling the former, and the tail and claws like those of the latter: he asserts it would attack all other animals, but was never known to hurt a man; that sometimes it would carry its prey on its back, and when it had eaten till satisfied, it concealed the rest under the leaves, or other cover; that every animal dreaded it to such a degree, that they would not touch any part of the prey it had left; and that the Indians called it Michibichi, which is an animal of the species of the tiger, but smaller and less speckled, and is now known to be the panther.

The beaver is a curious animal, but it has been described by so many authors, that I shall only observe what I believe they have not yet mentioned.—It is seldom seen in the day time: After sun set it leaves its habitation, and ventures abroad either to work, or procure food. It also takes this opportunity to wash itself. But the most remarkable singularity of this animal, is, that it lies with its tail constantly in the water, to prevent its getting stiff. The flesh of it is very good, either

G

boiled or roasted, but the tail is the best part. While I am upon the subject of dainties, I may add, that the snout of the moose is also highly esteemed. Not any of the animals in North America are to be dreaded, except the grizzled bear, which generally keeps in as warm a climate as possible: wherever it comes it makes dreadful havock, destroying men, and even frequently whole families.

During the time I stayed at Michillimakinac, a remarkable circumstance of bravery and generosity was communicated to me, which may not be unentertaining to the reader.

An Indian boy, about fifteen years of age, was standing at some distance from the fort, when a Savage fired his gun, and accidentally killed an Englishman. As he was advancing, he discovered the boy leaning against a tree, and not being of the same nation, he formed the resolution of taking him prisoner: having no suspicion of the boy's intention, he went up to him, and took him by the arm; the boy very artfuly drew back, and shot the Indian through the chin: this so incensed him, that he was raising his hand to tomahawk him, when another Indian instantly coming up, asked his companion who had wounded him? he replied, the boy, adding, that he would immediately take his scalp: the other prevented his bloody purpose, and told him he would protect the lad, for he was too brave to die. He carried him to the fort, where he was purchased by the commanding officer, to prevent the Indian whom he had wounded from killing him.

Description of LAKE SUPERIOR, *with the Ceremony of Indian Adoption.*

HAVING taken in Indian corn, and hard grease, (the food all traders carry to the upper country) and exchanged my large canoes, or maître canots, for smaller ones, the latter being more convenient to transport across the carrying places, and better calculated to run into small creeks, we proceeded to the Falls of St. Mary, (a strait so called) which is formed by two branches that separate from each other at the furthest point of the lake. Here is a small picketted fort built by the Indians, and about ten log houses for the residence of English and French traders. The nation of the Sauteurs formerly were settled at the foot of the Falls, and the Jesuits had a house near them. At this place there is abundance of fine fish, particularly pickerill, trout, and white fish of an uncommon size. From this place we continued our voyage to Lake Superior, formerly called Lake Tracy, in honour of Mons. de Tracy, who was appointed viceroy of America by the French king in June, 1665. It is reckoned six hundred leagues in circumference, and on it are a great number of large and small islands. At the entrance of this lake is a high rock, somewhat in the shape of a man, which the Chippeway Indians call "Kitchee Manitoo," or the Master of Life. Here they all stop to make their offerings, which they do by throwing tobacco, and other things, into the water: by this they intend to make an acknowledgment to the rock, as the representative of the Supreme Being, for the blessings they enjoy, cheerfully sacrificing to him their ornaments, and those things which they hold most dear. An example worthy of imitation, so far as respects the good intention of the creature to the Creator, exhibiting an evident proof that man in his natural state, without any of the refinements of civilization, is sensible of his dependance on an invisible power, however ignorantly, or unworthily, he may express his belief. God alone knoweth the heart, and will judge every man by the knowledge he hath.

Superstition is a noxious plant, but it hath flourished in every climate from the torrid to the frigid zone. If its effects have proved so pernicious among civilized nations, as we know they have, is it to be wondered that barbarians have suffered by it? The poor untutored Indian will not incur a great degree of censure for obeying the dictates of his uninformed nature, and following implicitly the custom of his ancestors. Revealed religion has not been given to all, and it is a melancholy reflection that those who have been enlightened by it, are not so superior to the Savages as one should naturally expect to find them.

In this rock there are several cavities near a mile in length, and about twenty feet in width, arched at the top. The lake freezes only close to the shore, the water being constantly in a swell, and the waves frequently mountains high, which is easily accounted for, when we consider its immense extent. On a calm day, a little distance from shore, sturgeon may be seen in very deep water. The surrounding land is high and rocky, and the woods extremely thick. The palm, birch, ash, spruce, and cedar, grow large, and in great abundance. The North-west Company, established at Montreal, keep a vessel on the lake to transport their goods from Michillimakinac to the grand portage on the north-west side, and return with the peltry collected in the inlands.

On the 4th of July we arrived at Pays Plat, on the north east side of the Lake, where we unpacked our goods, and made the bales smaller, having, by the Indian accounts, one hundred and eighty carrying places to the part where I intended to winter. On our landing we discovered at some distance a number of Indians, which induced us to accelerate the arrangement of the cargo, in case of barter, and be prepared to embark when the business was finished. Every thing being properly secured, I made up to the Savages, and calculated their number at one hundred and fifty: most of them were of the Chippeway tribes; the rest were of the nation of the Wasses. They gave me fish, dried meat, and skins, which I returned with trifling presents. The chief, whose name was Matchee Quewish, held a council, and finding I understood their language, proposed to adopt me as a brother warrior. Though I had not undergone this ceremony, I was not entirely ignorant of the nature of it, having been informed by other traders of the pain they endured in their adoption, though they declared they were favoured exceedingly; I determined however to submit to it, lest my refusal of the honour intended me should be attributed to fear, and so render me unworthy of the esteem of those from whom I expected to derive great advantages, and with whom I had engaged to continue for a considerable time.

The ceremony of adoption is as follows.———A feast is prepared of dog's flesh boiled in bear's grease, with huckle berries, of which it is expected every one should heartily partake. When the repast is over, the war song is sung in the following words.

" Master of Life, view us well; we receive a brother warrior who " appears to have sense, shews strength in his arm, and does not refuse " his body to the enemy."

After-the war song, if the person does not discover any signs of fear, he is regarded with reverence and esteem; courage, in the opinion of the Savages, being considered not only as indispensible, but as the greatest recommendation. He is then seated on a beaver robe, and presented with a pipe of war to smoke, which is put round to every warrior, and a wampum belt is thrown over his neck.

The calumet, or Indian pipe, which is much larger than that the Indians usually smoke, is made of marble, stone, or clay, either red, white, or black, according to the custom of the nation, but the red is mostly esteemed; the length of the handle is about four feet and a half, and made of strong cane, or wood, decorated with feathers of various colours, with a number of twists of female hair interwoven in different forms; the head is finely polished; two wings are fixed to it, which make it in appearance not unlike to Mercury's wand. This calumet is the symbol of peace, and the Savages hold it in such estimation, that a violation of any treaty where it has been introduced, would in their opinion be attended with the greatest misfortunes.

Wampum is of several colours, but the white and black are chiefly used; the former is made of the inside of the conque, or clam shell;

the latter of the muscle: both are worked in the form of a long bead, and perforated in order to their being strung on leather, and made up in belts.

These belts are for various purposes: When a council is held, they are given out with the speeches, and always proportioned in their size, and the number of the rows of wampum which they contain, to the idea the Indians entertain of the importance of the meeting; they frequently consist of both colours. Those given to Sir William Johnson, of immortal Indian memory, were in several rows, black on each side, and white in the middle: the white being placed in the centre, was to express peace, and that the path between them was fair and open. In the centre of the belt was the figure of a diamond, made of white wampum, which the Indians call the council fire.

When Sir William Johnson held a treaty with the Savages, he took the belt by one end, while the Indian chief held the other: if the chief had any thing to say, he moved his finger along the white streak; if Sir William had any thing to communicate, he touched the diamond in the middle.

These belts are also the records of former transactions, and being worked in particular forms, are easily deciphered by the Indians, and referred to in every treaty with the white people. When a string or belt of wampum is returned, it is a proof that the proposed treaty is not accepted, and the negotiation is at an end.

But to return from this digression. When the pipe has gone round, a sweating-house is prepared with six long poles fixed in the ground, and pointed at the top; it is then covered with skins and blankets to exclude the air, and the area of the house will contain only three persons. The person to be adopted is then stripped naked, and enters the hut with two chiefs; two large stones made red hot are brought in, and thrown on the ground; water is then brought in a bark dish, and sprinkled on the stones with cedar branches, the steam arising from which puts the person into a most profuse perspiration, and opens the pores to receive the other part of the ceremony.

When the perspiration is at the height, he quits the house, and jumps into the water; immediately on coming out a blanket is thrown over him, and he is led to the chief's hut, where he undergoes the following operation. Being extended on his back, the chief draws the figure he intends to make with a pointed stick, dipped in water in which gunpowder has been dissolved; after which, with ten needles dipped in vermilion, and fixed in a small wooden frame, he pricks the delineated parts, and where the bolder outlines occur, he incises the flesh with a gun flint; the vacant spaces, or those not marked with vermilion, are rubbed in with gunpowder, which produces the variety of red and blue; the wounds are then seared with pink wood, to prevent them from festering.

This operation, which is performed at intervals, lasts two or three days. Every morning the parts are washed with cold water, in which is infused an herb called Pockqueesegan, which resembles English box, and is mixed by the Indians with the tobacco they smoke, to take off the strength. During the process, the war songs are sung, accompanied by a rattle hung round with hawk bells, called chessaquoy, which is kept shaking, to stifle the groans such pains must naturally occasion. Upon the ceremony being completed, they give the party a name; that which they allotted to me, was *Amik*, or Beaver.

In return for the presents given me by Matchee Quewish, which I had only acknowledged by some trinkets, and to shew how much I was pleased with the honour they had conferred on me, I resolved to add to my former gifts; I accordingly took the chiefs to a spot where I had directed my men to place the goods intended for them, and gave them scalping knives, tomahawks, vermilion, tobacco, beads, &c. and lastly rum, the *unum necessarium*, without which (whatever else had been bestowed on them) I should have incurred their serious displeasure. Our canoes being turned up, and the goods properly secured, I told the Canadians to keep a constant watch, night and day, while we were encamped. This precaution is absolutely necessary, as the Indians generally do mischief when they are intoxicated. On this occasion our care was of infinite service, for with the rum we gave them, they continued in a state of inebriety three days and nights, during which frolic they killed four of their own party; one of whom was a great chief, and was burnt by his son: having been a famous warrior, he was buried with the usual honours peculiar to the Savages, viz. a scalping knife, tomahawk, beads, paint, &c. some pieces of wood to make a fire, and a bark cup to drink out of in his journey to the other country.

On the 21st we embarked, leaving the band extremely well satisfied with our conduct, which they acknowledged in the most expressive language; but as it was customary to take conductors from one Lake to another, I engaged twenty of the Chippeways to accompany me in passing by land the Grande Côte de la Roche, which is the rout that all the traders are obliged to take, on account of the great cataract, which is reckoned six hundred feet in height at the entrance of the Nipegon River. This journey is extremely fatiguing to the men, who are obliged to ascend a steep hill with considerable burdens, and for this reason it is customary to rest two or three days to recruit their strength.

We left la Grande Côte de la Roche in good spirits, and continued our voyage to Lake Alemipigon, where we met another band of Savages of the same nation. A council was held, and mutual presents exchanged. We stayed here ten days, encamped by the side of the Lake; during which time a skirmish happened among the Indians, in which three men were killed, and two wounded, after a dreadful scene of riot and confusion, occasioned by the baneful effects of rum.

Lake Alemipigon, or Nipegon, is about one hundred miles in length, and supplies the Savages with great quantities of fish. The land affords abundance of wild roots, and the animals are very numerous. The Indians who hunt here are in number about three hundred, and are remarkably wild and superstitious.

On the first of August we departed with fifteen Indians, not only to serve as guides, but to assist us across the portages. We lived on animal food and roots, reserving our corn and hard grease for the winter. Every evening at sun set we encamped, and got into our canoes at break of day. We continued our march to Lac Eturgeon, or Sturgeon Lake, but did not stay there a sufficient time to enable me to give a particular account of it; I have, however, described it in the narrative of my journey to Lake Manontoye, where I encamped for three days on account of the badness of the weather.

On the twenty fifth of September we arrived at Lac la Mort, or Dead Lake, situate to the north-east of Lake Alemipigon. This Lake is about sixty miles in circumference, the land low and swampy, and the water very unpleasant to the palate: it has been much frequented by the Indians, for, during the time I wintered there, I discovered no less than thirty-five different roads, about three feet wide, leading from the woods to the Lake side: it abounds with fish, and is frozen over in the winter, the ice not breaking away till April. The Indians who resort to it are good hunters, but very wild. The Chippeways are not so fond of dress as the other Savages, particularly those tribes who live very remote from Michillimakinac; this is easily accounted for; as the ice remains almost to the last spring month in England, and the winter season begins early in the month of October, the intermediate time is employed in making and repairing canoes, taking short excursions for food, amusing themselves in swimming, and other pastimes peculiar to the Savages. The luxury of dress can be little regarded by those whose constant necessities require the utmost exertions for their daily supply, and who are not provident enough to lay up a store of provisions for winter. Indians in general are extremely indolent, from the wildest to the most civilized, and value themselves upon being so; conceiving it beneath the dignity of a warrior to labour, and that all domestic cares and concerns are the province of women alone. This aversion for labour does not arise from dread, or dislike of fatigue; on the contrary, no people encounter or endure it with more chearfulness, particularly in their amusements, which are of various kinds, and many of them violent and laborious. They are calculated to make them athletic, and at the same time by the profuse perspiration with they occasion, they render the joints supple, and enable them to hunt with more facility.

Playing at ball, which is a favourite game, is very fatiguing. The ball is about the size of a cricket ball, made of deer skin, and stuffed with hair; this is driven forwards and backwards with short sticks, about two feet long, and broad at the end like a bat, worked like a racket, but with larger interstices: by this the ball is impelled, and from the elasticity of the racket, which is composed of deers' sinews, is thrown to a great distance: the game is played by two parties, and the contest lies in intercepting each other, and striking the ball into a goal, at the distance of about four hundred yards, at the extremity of which are placed two high poles, about the width of a wicket from each other; the victory consists in driving the ball between the poles. The Indians play with great good humour, and even when one of them happens, in the heat of the game, to strike another with his stick, it is not resented. But these accidents are cautiously avoided, as the violence with which they strike has been known to break an arm or a leg.

Atbtergain, or miss none but catch all, is also a favourite amusement with them, in which the women frequently take a part. It is played with a number of hard beans, black and white, one of which has small spots, and is called the king: they are put into a shallow wooden bowl, and shaken alternately by each party, who sit on the ground opposite to one another; whoever is dexterous enough to make the spotted bean jump out of the bowl, receives of the adverse party as many beans as there are spots: the rest of the beans do not count for any thing.

The boys are very expert at *trundling a hoop*, particularly the Cahnuaga Indians, whom I have frequently seen excel at this amusement. The game is played by any number of boys who may accidentally assemble together, some driving the hoop, while others with bows and arrows shoot at it. At this exercise they are surprisingly expert, and will stop the progress of the hoop when going with great velocity, by driving the pointed arrow into its edge; this they will do at a considerable distance, and on horseback as well as on foot. They will also kill small birds at fifty yards distance, and strike a halfpenny off a stick at fifteen yards. Spears and tomahawks they manage with equal dexterity.

Settlement at Lac la Mort, with the Proceedings of a Trading Party.

THE fatigue my Canadians had undergone rendered it necessary to prepare for wintering, and induced me to settle at Lac la Mort. The weather was also setting in cold, and threatened to be very severe, which was an additional motive. Having refreshed ourselves, and secured the canoes, I took two Indians to shew me a spot proper for building upon. We fixed close to the lake side, where we erected a loghouse, thirty feet long, and twenty feet wide, divided into two apartments, into which we deposited our goods. The next concern was to conceal our canoes in the woods, and to hide the rum under ground, except a small quantity for immediate use, knowing by experience the necessity of keeping it from the Indians, as our safety so essentially depended on it.

Having arranged every domestic concern, and spread our table in the wilderness, we prepared our winter firing, as wood is very difficult to bring home in severe weather. At leisure times we hunted, to increase our stock of provisions, which would not have been sufficient to support our household, and not choosing to risk the uncertainty of the arrival of Savages, who sometimes bring animal food to the traders. As the snow began to fall very heavy, we were prevented from making long excursions, without using snow shoes. For the space of a fortnight we hunted with great success, and caught a number of small animals, on which we feasted daily; these proved a seasonable relief, and saved the corn and grease. We had been settled about three weeks, when a large band of Savages arrived; having only eight Canadians with me, I desired them to act with the utmost precaution, as our number was comparatively small, and in case of a drunken frolic, the property might be pillaged, and our lives sacrificed: fortunately for me I had very steady men, who were well accustomed to the Northwest Indians. We were mutually pleased with each other, as no trader had wintered there before. The great chief, whose name was *Kesconcek*, made me a present of skins, dried meat, fish, and wild oats; a civility which I returned without delay, and in a manner with which he seemed highly gratified. The rest of the Savages then came into my house, one by one, which is called Indian file, singing war songs, and dancing. All of them, except the chief, placed themselves on the ground; he, standing upright with great dignity in the centre of the tribe, delivered the following speech.

" *Angaymer Nocey, wa baguamissey kaygo arwayyor hee zargetoone*
" *oway bartbtyage Nisbinnorbay nogome cawwickca kitcbee Artawway*
" *winnin, kitcbee morgussey cargoneek neennerwind zargetoone artaw-*
" *way neennerwind debwoye Nocey bartbtyage meekintargan omar ap-*
" *peemeenequy, mackquab, amik, warbesbance menoacb hegonce.*"——
" It is true, Father, I and my young men are happy to see you:—as
" the great Master of Life has sent a trader to take pity on us Savages,
" we shall use our best endeavours to hunt and bring you wherewithal
" to satisfy you in furs, skins, and animal food."

This speech was in fact intended to induce me to make them further presents; I indulged them in their expectations, by giving them two kegs of rum of eight gallons each, lowered with a small proportion of water, according to the usual custom adopted by all traders, five carrots of tobacco, fifty scalping knives, gun-flints, powder, shot, ball, &c. To the women I gave beads, trinkets, &c. and to eight chiefs who were in the band, each a North-west gun, a callico shirt, a scalping knife of the best sort, and an additional quantity of ammunition. These were received with a full yo-hah, or demonstration of joy.

The women, who are on all occasions slaves to their husbands, were ordered to make up bark huts, which they completed in about an hour, and every thing was got in order for merriment. The rum being taken from my house, was carried to their wigwaum, and they began to drink. The frolic lasted four days and nights; and notwithstanding all our precaution (securing their guns, knives, and tomahawks) two boys were killed, and six men wounded by three Indian women; one of the chiefs was also murdered, which reduced me to the necessity of giving several articles to bury with him, to complete the usual ceremony of their interment. These frolics are very prejudicial to all parties, and put the trader to a considerable expence, which nevertheless he cannot with safety refuse. On the fifth day they were all sober, and expressed great sorrow for their conduct, lamenting bitterly the loss of their friends.

On the 26th of October they departed for the hunt, which gave us great satisfaction, as we had scarcely rested during their abode with

us. When they got into their canoes, they sung the dead war song.—
" *Wabindam, Kitchee Maunitoo, baguarmissey bapitch neatissum :*"—
or, " Master of Life, view me well, you have given me courage to open
" my veins."

Having piled the winter's firing at a convenient distance from the
house to prevent accidents, we prepared the nets for fishing. The ice
was three feet thick, and the snow very deep; this we were obliged to
clear away, before we could cut holes in which to put our nets. For
the space of two months we had uncommon success, having caught
about eighteen hundred weight of fish, which we hung up by the tails
across sticks to freeze, and then laid them up for store. This was to
us an important acquisition, as fishing in the middle of winter is precarious, and the return of the Indians to supply the wants of the traders
very uncertain.

In summer the fishers go up the lakes, as well as rivers, and are generally most successful at the foot of a deep stream, or the mouth of a
creek. In the beginning of winter they cut a large opening, and set
nets. In the depth of winter they make a small hole, in which they
angle; and sometimes they cut two holes in a right line through the ice,
and pass a line at the end of a stick from hole to hole, by which they
haul the net under the ice, frequently with good success. In winter,
fishing is the daily employ of half the men, though in very severe weather it is a fatiguing service.

In the beginning of January, 1778, our provisions run short,
having nothing left but some spawn of fish, which we beat up with

warm water and lived upon. The intense severity of the weather would not allow us to look after the nets; and although thus distressed for want of better food, we were obliged to stay at home, keeping a large fire, and lying almost continually on our blankets, which weakened us exceedingly. Having remained in this inactive state for some time, and hunger pressing hard, I roused myself, and proposed to my men to make marten traps, which they went about with the utmost cheerfulness. When they had finished a sufficient number, they set them in the woods, at the distance of about two miles from the house. While they were employed in this service, I was left alone, it being necessary for some one to remain, in case of the arrival of Savages. The first day my men were successful, and returned with two racoons, three hares, and four musquashes; on these we feasted the next day; and though we were not satisfied, they proved a seasonable relief, and enabled us to pursue the business we were engaged in with greater spirits, fondly expecting more prosperous days.

In a little time we were again destitute, and the men became disheartened; this induced me to propose a journey to Lake Manontoye, where we knew Mr. Shaw, a brother trader, had wintered, to endeavour to procure some wild rice, which the Indians told me grew in the swamps at that place. The Canadians approved of the plan, and said they hoped they should be able to provide for their subsistence till my return. Previous to my departure, we were compelled to kill a favourite dog, belonging to Joseph Boneau, one of my people, which most sensibly affected us, because, independent of the attachment we had towards him, he was a very useful animal. The next morning I put on my snow shoes, and persuaded an Indian and his wife, who were with me occasionally, and had accidentally come in from the hunt with six hares, to accompany me, promising them payment in rum at my return: they agreed to go, and it was very fortunate they did, as I could not have found the way without a guide.

We set off with the six hares, and travelled four days without killing any thing; this was a disappointment, but with the little stock we carried with us, we subsisted tolerably well. About an hour before sunset on the fourth day, we stopped at a small creek, which was too deep to be forded, and whilst the Indian was assisting me in making a raft to cross over, rather than swim through in such cold weather, against a strong current, I looked round, and missed his wife: I was rather displeased, as the sun was near setting, and I was anxious to gain the opposite shore, to encamp before dark. I asked the Indian where she was gone; he smiled, and told me, he supposed into the woods to set a collar for a partridge. In about an hour she returned with a new-born infant in her arms, and coming up to me, said in Chippeway, " *Oway* "*Saggonasb Paysbik Sbomagonisb*," or, " Here, Englishman, is a young " warrior." It is said that the Indian women bring forth children with very little pain, but I believe it is merely an opinion. It is true they are strong and hardy, and will support fatigue to the moment of their delivery; but this does not prove they are exempt from the common feelings of the sex on such trying occasions. A young woman of the Rat Nation has been known to be in labour a day and a night, without a groan. The force of example acting upon their pride, will not allow these poor creatures to betray a weakness, or express the pain they feel, probably lest the husband should think her unworthy of his future attention, and despise both mother and child: at any rate, he would tell her the infant, if a boy, would never be a warrior; and if a girl, would have a dastardly spirit, and of course neither of them be fit for a Savage life.

I believe it will not be disputed that the Indian women love their children with as much affection as parents in the most civilized states can boast; many proofs might be adduced to support this assertion. A mother suckles her child till it attains the age of four or five years, and sometimes till it is six or seven. From their infant state they endeavour to promote an independent spirit; they are never known either to beat or scold them, lest the martial disposition which is to adorn their future life and character, should be weakened: on all occasions they avoid every thing compulsive, that the freedom with which they wish them to think and act may not be controuled. If they die, they lament their death with unfeigned tears, and even for months after their decease will weep at the graves of their departed children. The nation of Savages called Biscatonges, or by the French, Pleureurs, are said to weep more bitterly at the birth of a child, than at its decease; because they look upon death only as a journey from whence he will return, but with regard to his birth, they consider it as an entrance into a life of perils and misfortunes.

As soon as a child is born, if in summer, the mother goes into the water, and immerses the infant; as soon as this is done, it is wrapped up in a small blanket, and tied to a flat board, covered with dry moss, in the form of the bottom of a coffin, with a hoop over the top, where the head lies, to preserve it from injury. In winter it is clad in skins as well as blankets. In the heat of summer gauze is thrown over the young Savage, to keep off the musquitoes, which are very troublesome in the woods. The board, on which the child is placed, is slung to the mother's forehead with a broad worsted belt, and rests against her back.

When the French took possession of Canada, the women had neither linen, nor swaddling cloaths; all their child-bed furniture consisted of a kind of trough, filled with dry rotten wood dust, which is as soft as the finest down, and well calculated to imbibe the moisture of the infant; on this the child was placed, covered with rich furs, and tied down with strong leather strings. The dust was changed as often as necessary, till the child was weaned.

Among the Indians who are in any degree civilized, the women feed their children with pap made of Indian corn and milk, if it can be obtained; but in the parts more northern, and remote from Europeans, wild rice and oats are substituted, which being cleansed from the husk, and pounded between two stones, are boiled in water with maple sugar: this food is reckoned very nourishing, and with broth made from the flesh of animals and fish, which they are frequently able to procure, cannot fail of supporting and strengthening the infant. Among several of the tribes of Indians, pap is made of sagavite, from a root they call toquo, of the bramble kind; this is washed and dried, afterwards ground, or pounded, and made into a paste, which being baked is pleasant to the taste, but of a very astringent quality. It is their common bread.

On our arrival at Lac Eturgeon, as the weather was bad, we encamped three days, which gave me an opportunity of making some observations on this Lake, which I could not do when I passed it in my way to Lac la Mort.

This Lake, by the Indian accounts, is about five days journey by water: the width in some parts is about thirty miles. There are a number of small islands on it which abound with hares, partridges, and wild fowl. The Indians who frequent it are the Hawoyzask or Musquash, who speak the Chippeway language. They are usually more stationary than the generality of the Chippeways; they seldom leave the inlands, and are excellent hunters. Mr. Carver, in his chart, points out a village leading to Riviére St. 'Croix, which he says belongs to the roving Chippeways; but I believe all the nation, with very few exceptions, may be called rovers in the strictest sense of the word.

The first day of our encampment we killed a hare, made fish-hooks of the thigh bones, and baited them with the flesh. The lines were made of the bark of the willow tree cut into slips, and twisted hard together. Success crowned our endeavours, for we not only caught sufficient for present use, but enough for the remainder of the journey to Lake Manontoye.

The day before our arrival we killed two otters, which I intended as a present to Mr. Shaw, not doubting but any animal food would be acceptable from the severity of the season, concluding that his situation was as bad as our own, except in the article of wild oats. When arrived within about six miles of the lake, we met a small party of Indians, who alarmed us by an account of a dreadful confusion among their tribe, occasioned by the Hudson's Bay Savages having killed three of their band; and they said they believed Mr. Shaw had fallen a sacrifice to their fury, as they had heard them consult together to plunder the trader. They lamented exceedingly their inability to assist him, not being even strong enough to resent their own personal injury; however, they promised to accompany me on the way, as near to Mr. Shaw's house as their safety would admit.

Having taken refreshment, we pursued our journey till within two miles of the house, when they thought it prudent to leave me, and wishing me success, retired into the woods, out of the track, to avoid being seen, where they promised to stay till my return. My Indian and his wife did not choose to proceed any farther, being also afraid of the Hudson's Bay Savages. I confess my situation was very unpleasant, and I debated in my mind what steps to take to attempt the relief of a brother trader, and at the same time avoid injury myself. Relying on my usual success in suppressing these kind of tumults occasioned by intoxication, and conscious that I knew as well as any man the nature of the Indians when under its pernicious influence, I did not doubt, however unsuccessful my endeavours might prove as to rescuing Mr. Shaw from his perilous situation, but that I should certainly be able to effect an escape myself in case of an attack; and as one favourable suggestion frequently gives birth to another, and establishes by degrees a confidence in the mind, I anticipated Mr. Shaw's delivery to my entire satisfaction. Fortified by these flattering hopes, I determined to exert my best and speediest endeavours in his behalf, and pursued my journey without delay. When I arrived within a quarter of a mile of the scene of discord, I heard the war-hoop in a manner very loud and clamorous; and though I had been accustomed

VOYAGES AND TRAVELS.

to such sounds, I was very much alarmed, and felt my resolution rather staggered; sensible that the rage of drunken Indians, when it has risen to a certain pitch, knows no bounds, and of the extreme difficulty of reconciling them to any person to whom they had unfortunately taken a dislike. Animated, however, with the idea of behaving like a warrior, and recurring to the time when I was adopted at Pays Plat, I conceived it unmanly to shrink from danger, and pushing through the woods, had soon a full view of the infernal spirits, for I could give them no better name.

I lay some minutes in ambush, listening with great attention, till I heard one of them cry out in the Chippeway language, "*Haguarmissey mornooch gunnisar Cusbecance;*" or, "I do not mean to kill "the *Cat*;" which was a name given to Mr. Shaw by the Indians, from his speaking in a feeble voice. This convinced me he was alive, though in imminent danger. I made all possible haste up to the house, and found the Savages, both men and women, completely drunk. The huts had been knocked down, the canoes adrift, and the whole formed the most dreadful scene of confusion I had ever beheld. There were also an old Indian and a woman, who I afterwards learned was his mother, lying dead upon the snow by the lake side. I made several efforts to get into the house, but was prevented by the Savages, who kept me back, kissing me, and telling me they loved me, but that I must not attempt to relieve the *Cat*. At last, with inconceivable difficulty, I persuaded them to attend to me, and felt the most extreme satisfaction in having succeeded, at least so far, in an attempt which would have been dangerous to any one to have undertaken who was not fully master of the language and character of the Savages, and at the same time cool and dispassionate enough to hear their nonsense with patience and temper.

I then addressed myself to the most sober of the chiefs, and inquired of him the cause of the dispute; he told me Mr. Shaw was a *dog* instead of a *cat*, for that he had refused them rum; and that though he and the rest of the tribe were happy to see me, because they had heard I always had a good heart towards the Savages, I should not go in to assist the trader, for they were the masters of the wigwaum, and not he, and that they were resolved to have all the rum in his possession before break of day.

Mr. Shaw's house might very properly be styled a fort, being secured by high pickets, which made it difficult for the Indians to approach it, and he had taken the precaution to fasten the outer gate as well as the door. I told the chief it was not my intention to interfere, that I passed accidentally in my way to Lac le Rouge, and should only stay to refresh myself. This information pleased him exceedingly, as he knew Mr. Shaw had only one man in the house, the rest, with the interpreter, being out in search of provisions, so that at my departure there would not remain force sufficient to obstruct their proceedings. I perceived them so fully bent on accomplishing their purpose, that had I betrayed the least intention or inclination to relieve the unhappy man, I should most probably have been dispatched without much ceremony. The effects of the rum they had already drank, had so elevated their spirits, that nothing less than the full possession of the whole stock would satisfy them; and I am persuaded that if half of them had perished, the rest would without hesitation have risked their lives in the attempt. To avoid all suspicion,

K

which would probably have been fatal both to Mr. Shaw and myself, I left the chief, and watched an opportunity of returning undiscovered. Fortunately the Indians had not drank all the rum Mr. Shaw had given them, and the chief as soon as I had left him went back to his hut to increase his intoxication, and communicate the conversation which passed between us, the rest of the band having retired soon after the conference began.

Observing the coast clear, I walked unobserved to the fort, and spoke loud both in French and English: Mr. Shaw and his man heard me, and recollecting my voice, were transported beyond measure. The man, who was a Canadian, was most delighted, as his fears were very strong, it being the first year he had wintered among the Savages. On my approach, I heard him cry out with the greatest vehemence, " *Mon Dieu! que* " *je suis content! Nôtre ami est arrivé, autrement nous serions fou-* " *tu. Je conte assurément, que nous serons bientôt libre, mon cher* " *bourgeois.*" He instantly opened the gate; I entered precipitately, and congratulated him on the prospect of counteracting the designs of the Indians, being resolved to exert my best endeavours, and to live or die with them. Mr. Shaw thanked me for my professions of friendship, and immediately gave me a concise account of the disturbance. He said the Hudson's Bay Indians had come to him with very little peltry, and after trading for it, he had given them more rum than they had any right to expect; that instead of being content with this, they insisted on more; that in a fit of intoxication they had killed an Indian and his mother; and had attempted to set fire to his house with punk wood, which they shot at it lighted, fixed to the points of arrows. Having heard his story, I encouraged him to keep up his spirits, and advised him, when the Indians returned to execute their purpose, to appear indifferent to their menaces.

Whilst we were in deep discourse, I discovered three chiefs at a small distance from the house, in very earnest conversation, and was convinced they were devising some scheme to effect their design. As they approached, I called to them, and desired them to come into the house: they immediately advanced, and walked in one by one, with looks of treachery, which the earnestness of the business to be executed would not allow them to conceal. I talked to them without the least reserve, and in apparent good temper: I asked them if they were sober; but before they could give me an answer, the rest of the band came to the door, but did not enter; the head chief then told me they were very sober, and expressed great concern for their conduct, but that now the strong water had lost its influence, they saw their folly, and were sure the bad spirit had left their hearts.

I told them the Master of Life was angry with them, and that they did not deserve success in hunting, for their bad behaviour to the trader, who had been a kind father to them, and supplied all their wants. I then presented them with some tobacco to smoke in council, which was well received, and looking earnestly at the chief, addressed the band to the following effect.

" *Keennerwind Ojemar woke, kee wabindan indenendum kee kee*
" *noneydone Kitcbee Mannitoo, ojey candan opin weene aighter ojey*
" *petoone nowwetting guyack debarchemon kaygait nin oathty bapadgey*
" *nee woke keennerwind equoy kee janis goyer metach nogome gudder-*

" *barchemon bunjyta O, nisbsbishshin artawway winnin kaygait nee*
" *zargetoone artawway winnin metach hakaygo arwayyor Matchee Man-*
" *nitoo, guyyack neennerwind oathly mornooch kee appay omar neegee.*"

" You chiefs, and others of the tribe whose eyes are open, I hope
" you will give ear to the words of my mouth. The Master of Life has
" opened my brain, and made my breath blow good words. My heart
" feels for you, your wives, and children; and what I now speak pro-
" ceeds from the root of my friend's sentiments, who owns this house,
" and who has told me that his heart was opened to you on your arrival;
" but notwithstanding his kindness, the bad spirit got possession of you,
" which made him very unhappy, though he hoped the Master of Life
" would change your dispositions, and make you good Indians, as you
" used to be." To this speech one of the chiefs made answer:

" *Kaygait Amik, kee aighter annaboycassey omar bapadgey; O, nish-*
" *shishshin kee debarchemon nogome neennerwind ojey stootewar cockin-*
" *nor nee doskeennerwaymug kee debwoye neccarnis bapadgey sannegat*
" *neennerwind ha nishinnorbay kaygwotch annaboycassey oxome Scuttay-*
" *wabo ojey minniquy neennerwind angaymer Amik, shashyyea sugger-*
" *marsh cockinnor nogome mornooch towarch payshik muccuk Scuttay-*
" *wabo ojey bockettynan Cushshecance warbunk keejayp neennerwind ojey*
" *boossin ;—baw, baw, baw.*"

" It is true, Beaver, you have strong sense, it sweetens your words
" to us, and we all understand you. We know, friend, your lips open
" with truth. It is very hard for us Indians, who have not the sense
" of the white people to know when we have had enough of the strong

VOYAGES AND TRAVELS.

"fiery water; but we hope the *Cat* will throw off the film from his heart,
"as ours are clear: we also hope he will open his heart once more, and
"give us a small keg of the strong water, to drink to the health of our
"brother and sister, whom we have sent to the far country, and to-
"morrow at break of day we will depart."

Mr. Shaw, by my advice, promised to comply with their request, on condition of their being true to their engagements, and that they should forbear even tasting the rum while they remained on the ground. This determination I acquainted them with, and they retired to their huts, leaving us in quiet possession of the fort.

The Indians remained quiet all night, which induced me to hope that my promise of rum to them, on their departure, had accomplished the desired effect: but I flattered myself too much, as the storm was not yet even at the height. At break of day they assembled, and asked for the rum, which was immediately given them; and they got into their canoes, and went off without burying their dead. This being very uncustomary, alarmed me, as no people are more particular in paying the greatest respect to the remains of the deceased. Suspecting the bad spirit was still in them, and that they were only gone a short distance to drink the rum, we prepared for an attack, loading twenty eight north-west guns, and a brace of pistols, and sat down by the fire expecting their return to compleat the design my fortunate arrival had hitherto prevented. In about an hour they returned very much intoxicated, singing their dead war songs, and every warrior naked, painted black from head to foot: as they approached the house in Indian file, each one repeated the following words; " *Mornooch toworch gunnesar* "*cushsbecance neennerwind ojey dependan O wakaygan :*" or, " Nevertheless we do not mean to kill the *Cat*, we only own this fort, and all that is in it."

Whilst they were singing, we were preparing our guns, and placing them so as to be ready for immediate use, if necessary; being determined to make a vigorous resistance, although there remained only Mr. Shaw and myself, the Canadian having fled to the woods.

I assumed the character of commander in chief, and desired Mr. Shaw to obey my orders implicitly, and by no means to fire till I gave the signal; well knowing that the death of one of the Savages, even in our own defence, would so exasperate the rest that there would not be a possibility of escaping their fury. As our situation was truly critical, we acted with as much coolness as men devoted to destruction could. A fortunate thought came into my head, which I instantly put in practice: I went into the store, and rolling a barrel of gunpowder into the outer room, knocked out the head. I had scarcely finished it, before the Savages arrived, and advancing to the door, armed with spears and tomahawks, said to each other, "*keen etam,*" or, " you go first." We stood ready to receive them, and gave them to understand we were not afraid of them. One of the band entered the house, and I said to him sternly, "*Ha wa neyoe shemagonish equoy hee tertennin marmo?*" or, " Who now among you old women is a brave soldier?" and immediately pointing my pistol cocked to the barrel of gunpowder, cried out with great emphasis, "*Cochinnor marmo neepoo nogome ;*" or, " We will all die this day." On hearing these words they ran from the door, crying, "*Kitchee Mannitoo ojey petoone Amik O mushkowar baguarmissey yang :*"

or, "The Master of Life has given the Beaver great strength and courage." The women fled with the utmost precipitation, pushed their canoes into the water, and got off as fast as they could: the men, who before were intoxicated, became sober, and making as much haste as possible, paddled to an island opposite the house. Soon after a canoe came on shore with six women, to endeavour to make up the breach; but I refused all reconciliation, telling them that they might have known me before; that my name was Beaver; that all the Indians knew me to be a warrior; and that my heart was not easily melted. The women immediately returned, carrying with them the dead, which satisfied me they did not intend to trouble us again.

Thus, by an happy presence of mind, we were saved from almost inevitable destruction, and probably from ending our lives under the most excruciating torture.

It may not be improper to observe the necessity there is for a trader to be cool, firm, and, in case of emergency, brave, but not rash or hasty. The Indians are just observers of the human mind, and easily discover true from affected courage, by that apparent tranquillity which clearly distinguishes the former from the latter. It is well known that no people in the world put courage to so severe a trial, and watch at the executions of their enemies with such savage curiosity, the effects of the tortures they inflict; even the women exult in proportion to the agony betrayed by the unhappy sufferer; though it frequently happens thro' the same spirit operating on both parties, that the most excruciating torments cannot extort a sigh. An example or two from Mr. Adair's History of the American Indians, will shew the firmness of an Indian mind, and prove beyond a doubt that such anecdotes are not exaggerated. Truth should be the standard of history, and guide the pen of every author who values his reputation.

Some years ago the Shawano Indians being obliged to remove from their habitations, in their way took a Muskohge warrior, known by the name of old *Scrany*, prisoner; they bastinadoed him severely, and condemned him to the fiery torture. He underwent a great deal without shewing any concern; his countenance and behaviour were as if he suffered not the least pain. He told his persecutors with a bold voice, that he was a warrior; that he had gained most of his martial reputation at the expence of their nation, and was desirous of shewing them, in the act of dying, that he was still as much their superior, as when he headed his gallant countrymen against them: that although he had fallen into their hands, and forfeited the protection of the divine power by some impurity or other, when carrying the holy ark of war against his devoted enemies, yet he had so much remaining virtue as would enable him to punish himself more exquisitely than all their despicable ignorant crowd possibly could; and that he would do so, if they gave him liberty by untying him, and handing him one of the red hot gun-barrels out of the fire. The proposal, and his method of address, appeared so exceedingly bold and uncommon, that his request was granted. Then suddenly seizing one end of the red hot barrel, and brandishing it from side to side, he forced his way through the armed and surprised multitude, leaped down a prodigious steep and high bank into a branch of the river, dived through it, ran over a small island, and passed the other branch, amidst a shower of bullets; and though numbers of his enemies were in close pursuit of him, he got into a bramble swamp, through which, though naked and in a mangled condition, he reached his own country.

The Shawano Indians also captured a warrior of the Anantoocah nation, and put him to the stake, according to their usual cruel solemnities: having unconcernedly suffered much torture, he told them, with scorn, they did not know how to punish a noted enemy; therefore he was willing to teach them, and would confirm the truth of his assertion if they allowed him the opportunity. Accordingly he requested of them a pipe and some tobacco, which was given him; as soon as he had lighted it, he sat down, naked as he was, on the women's burning torches, that were within his circle, and continued smoking his pipe without the least discomposure: on this a head warrior leaped up, and said, they saw plain enough that he was a warrior, and not afraid of dying, nor should he have died, only that he was both spoiled by the fire, and devoted to it by their laws; however, though he was a very dangerous enemy, and his nation a treacherous people, it should be seen that they paid a regard to bravery, even in one who was marked with war streaks at the cost of many of the lives of their beloved kindred; and then, by way of favour, he with his friendly tomahawk instantly put an end to all his pains. Though the merciful but bloody instrument was ready some minutes before it gave the blow, yet I was assured, the spectators could not perceive the sufferer to change either his posture or his steadiness of countenance in the least.

Death, among the Indians, in many situations is rather courted than dreaded, and particularly at an advanced period of life, when they have not strength or activity to hunt: the father then solicits to change his climate, and the son cheerfully acts the part of an executioner, putting a period to his parent's existence.

Among the northern Chippeways, when the father of a family seems reluctant to comply with the usual custom, and his life becomes burdensome to himself and friends, and his children are obliged to maintain him with the labour of their hands, they propose to him the alternative, either to be put on shore on some island, with a small canoe and paddles, bows and arrows, and a bowl to drink out of, and there run the risk of starving; or to suffer death according to the laws of the nation, manfully. As there are few instances where the latter is not preferred, I shall relate the ceremony practised on such an occasion.

A sweating house is prepared in the same form as at the ceremony of adoption, and whilst the person is under this preparatory trial, the family are rejoicing that the Master of Life has communicated to them the knowledge of disposing of the aged and infirm, and sending them to a better country, where they will be renovated, and hunt again with all the vigour of youth. They then smoke the pipe of peace, and have their dog feast: they also sing the grand medicine song, as follows.

" *Wa baguarmissey Kitchee Mannitoo haygait cochinnor nisbinnorbay*
" *ojey kee candau bapadgey hee zargetoone nisbinnorbay mornooch hee*
" *tarpenan nocey keen aighter, O, dependan nisbinnorbay, mornooch tow-*
" *warch weene ojey mishcoot pochcan tunnockay.*——The Master of Life
" gives courage. It is true, all Indians know that he loves us, and

" we now give our father to him, that he may find himself young in
" another country, and be able to hunt."

The songs and dances are renewed, and the eldest son gives his father the death-stroke with a tomahawk: they then take the body, which they paint in the best manner, and bury it with the war weapons, making a bark hut to cover the grave, to prevent the wild animals from disturbing it.

Thus do the unenlightened part of mankind assume a privilege of depriving each other of life, when it can no longer be supported by the labour of their own hands, and think it a duty to put a period to the existence of those to whom they are indebted for their own, and employ those arms to give the fatal stroke, which, in more civilized countries, would have been exerted for their support.

I remained with Mr. Shaw until the return of his men, and took an Indian slay, loaded with wild rice and dried meat, and two of his Canadians to assist me. In my way I called at the place where I left the Indians who communicated to me the first account of the tumult at Mr. Shaw's, but they were gone. My Indian and his wife waited for me, and were rejoiced to see me again. On my return to Lac la Mort, I found all my men in good health and spirits, having been well supplied with provisions by the Savages, during my absence, and had increased my stock of peltry by barter. Mr. Shaw's men rested at my house one night, and the next morning set off for Manontoye.

Indian Manner of going to War, &c.

Lake Manontoye, where Mr. Shaw wintered, is not so large as Lac Eturgeon: it abounds with excellent fish and wild fowl; and oats, rice, and cranberries, grow spontaneously in the swamps. There are very few islands on it. There are about three hundred of the Chippeway nation who resort to it: they are very wild, and delight in war, which they sometimes wage against the Sioux, on the Mississippi; and they are frequently absent from their families fifteen months, scarce ever returning without a prisoner or a scalp.

It is very strange that the thirst of blood should stimulate the human mind to traverse such an amazing extent of country, suffering inexpressible hardships, and uncertain of success, to gratify a passion, which none but an infernal spirit could suggest; and when success has crowned his labours, that he should return with inconceivable satisfaction, and relate the transaction of his journey, with the greatest exultation, smiling at the relation of agonies which he alone occasioned. The most dreadful acts of a maniac cannot exceed such cruelty: happy those, who enjoy the benefits of society, whose civilization, and whose laws protect them from such detestable outrages.

Previous to their going to war, the head chief calls a council, and each chief has a belt of wampum, and a war pipe: the belt to remind them of former transactions relative to the nation they intend to commence hostilities against, and the pipe to smoke at the council fire. When they have determined to make war, they send the belts and pipes to their enemies; and if a similar compliment is returned, they instantly prepare for blood, with the most steady and determined resolution.

The novel of Emily Montague affords a striking example of this strong propensity for blood, which I shall relate in the author's own words.

" A Jesuit missionary told me a story on this subject, which one " cannot hear without horror. An Indian woman with whom he lived " on his mission, was feeding her children, when her husband brought " in an English prisoner; she immediately cut off his arm, and gave " her children the streaming blood to drink. The Jesuit remonstrated " on the cruelty of the action; on which, looking sternly at him—I " would have them warriors, said she, and therefore feed them with the " food of men."

When I was at Cataraqui, the capital of the Loyalist settlements in Canada, a party of Mohawks and Messesawgers accidentally met, and having bartered their skins and peltry with the traders, sat themselves down to drink the rum their merchandize had produced. As the liquor began to operate, their imaginations suggested to them that they were of different nations, and as the Mohawks always claimed a superiority, intoxication made them proud: at last a dispute arose, and a Messesawger Indian was killed, and his heart taken out, which the

Mohawks intended to have broiled, but they were prevented by a gentleman who accidentally passed by their hut, and prevailed upon them to give it up.

It seems to be the constant attention both of the male and female part of the Indians to instil ideas of heroism into the minds of the rising generation, and these impressions they carry far beyond the line of reason or of justice. Is it then surprising that every action of their lives should tend to satisfy their thirst for revenging offences committed against them, and that these sentiments should operate so powerfully in directing their future conduct? There is, nevertheless, one exception to these observations—their conduct to traders, who are obliged on some occasions, when intoxication runs high, to beat them very soundly;—to their credit, in these instances, I must confess I never knew them to resent this severity when sober. The only remark they have made has been—" Friend, you beat me very severely last night— " but I do not mind, I suppose I deserved it—it was the liquor made " me offend." Or if they betray any dissatisfaction, one glass of rum will reconcile all differences. With regard to severity when they are perfectly sober, I am convinced it would be highly dangerous, and should be cautiously avoided.

But although they often express these blood-thirsty sentiments, and too frequently put them in execution, yet there are occasions when they exercise both temper and reason.

When I was at Pimistiscotyan Landing, on Lake Ontario, I had a large dog, to protect myself and property; an Indian came in rather in liquor to ask for rum, and probably might strike the animal; the dog instantly seized him by the calf of the leg, and wounded him dreadfully. He returned to his hut, and made no complaint till the next morning, when he desired to speak with me: I went to him, and he told me how the dog had used him, saying, he hoped I would give him a pair of leggons, to supply those which the dog had torn; but that with regard to his leg, he did not trouble himself much about that, as he knew it would soon be well. I immediately granted his request, and added a bottle of rum, with which he seemed well pleased, and I heard no more of it.

But to return to the subject of going to war. The women and children sometimes go forward in their canoes singing the war songs, and encamp every evening at sun-set, having a great dislike to travelling in the dark. Forty-eight young warriors are placed, in four divisions, to keep guard at night, armed with guns, bows and arrows, and some scotté wigwas, or fire bark, to light in case of sudden surprise.

This bark is taken from the birch tree, and being properly dried, is used by the Indians to light them to spear fish: it is fixed on a stick about seven feet long, and either put at the head of the canoe, or carried by the person who attends upon the man that spears, and whose business it is also to steer the canoe.

At day break the Indians depart, and pursue their journey regardless of the weather, till they arrive in the enemy's country, when the utmost precaution is adopted that it is possible for human invention to suggest.

When war is made against the Mississippi Indians, they endeavour to kill the men and women, and bring away the children to dispose of to the traders, who send them down to Montreal for servants. The boys are not so much to be depended upon as the girls, being more stubborn, and naturally disdaining the idea of slavery; they are also full of pride and resentment, and will not hesitate to kill their masters in order to gratify their revenge for a supposed injury. The girls are more docile, and assimilate much sooner with the manners of civilization. Being unaccustomed to domestic life, they are at first sick and unhealthy; but the change soon becomes familiar to them, and they then prefer it to the uncultivated manner of living in which they were brought up.

A few days after my return to Lac la Mort, a band of Savages arrived from the Red Lake, called by the Indians, *Misqui Sahiegan*, and some from Lake Shabeechevan, or the Weed Lake, about five days march beyond Lake Manontoye. Red Lake is so called on account of a remarkable circumstance which happened to two famous warriors of the Chippeway nation, who were hunting by the lake side, and as they were looking out for game, perceived at some distance an enormous beast, that appeared much larger than any animal they had ever seen; his pace was slow and heavy, and he kept constantly by the water side. They followed him as close as they thought prudent, determined at all hazards to use their best endeavours to kill him. As they approached, they had a clearer view, and discovered that his body was covered with something like moss; this increased their surprise, and after consulting together, they continued advancing towards the beast, and fired large shot, without appearing to make any impression. They fired again with as little effect as before; then retreated some distance, sat down and sung their war songs, addressing themselves to the Master of Life, and desiring his assistance to enable them to conquer it, as they believed it to be the *Matchee Mannitoo*, or bad spirit, in the shape of this monster. They then got up and pursued him, both firing at the same time: the shot proved successful, and caused the animal to turn round, which induced them to keep up their fire till the beast jumped into the water, and they lost sight of him. From the circumstance of his blood dying the water red, this lake has ever since been called the Red Lake.

Fish is caught here in great abundance, and wild rice grows in very great plenty in the swamps. The country likewise abounds with all sorts of animals for hunting. There are several rivers and falls of water on the north-west part. The Indians are very fond of fishing and hunting here during the winter season, as they are generally very successful even in the most severe weather. From Red Lake to Lake le Sel, or Salt Lake, by the Indian accounts, there are fourteen short portages, and twenty-two creeks. Lake le Sel is very small, and the water shallow and muddy. It does not exceed three miles in length. There are few fish except eels, cat fish, and pike; but it abounds with musquashes and wild fowl. From this lake to Lake Caribou, or Rein-deer Lake, is eight days march across five creeks and three portages.

Lake Caribou, or, in the Indian language, *Ateeque*, is about thirty miles long, with several small islands, resembling the Mille Isles, in the River St. Laurence, above Montreal. The water is deep and clear,

M

and the bottom hard. It abounds with large trout, white fish, pickerill, pike, and sturgeon. It is surrounded by a chain of high mountains. Some years ago a French trader settled here, but of late it has been deserted. The Indians reckon it ten days march to Lake Schabeechevan, across thirteen portages, and as many creeks; but as I wintered here the following year, though I went to it by a different track, I shall not describe it till I give an account of the occurrences of that time. From Lake Schabeechevan to Lake Arbitibis are three small lakes, eight creeks, and five portages. Lake Arbitibis is very large, and the surrounding land rocky and mountainous. This Lake furnishes the Indians with fish and wild fowl. The aquatic race abound in this part of the world, doubtless so appointed for the support of the numerous tribes of Savages, who are obliged to resort to the lakes for food. At the northern extremity of this Lake is a large fall of water, which flows from a river whose current is rapid for about twenty miles. On this river there are also dangerous rapids; the land upon its banks is low, and the beach sandy. From Lake Arbitibis to Crow's-nest Lake, called by the Indians, *Cark Cark Sahiegan*, is a short distance. The utmost circumference of Crow's-nest Lake scarcely exceeds two leagues, and is only remarkable for a small island in the middle, with about forty high palm trees, where the crows build their nests, which is called *Cark Cark Minnesey*. The fish in this Lake are very indifferent, being mostly of the sword-fish kind, which the Indians seldom eat. From this Lake is a long portage, and about half way a high mountain. At the end of the carrying place is a river called *Cark Cark Seepi*, or Crows' River, which runs with a strong current for about thirty miles, from *Neesbsbemaince Sahiegan*, or the Lake of the Two Sisters; so called from the meeting of two currents, which form one grand discharge into the lake. The Hudson's Bay Indians hunt here with great success. At the end is a carrying place about a quarter of a mile long, that leads to a remarkably narrow river, which runs with a strong current for about fifty leagues: the land on each side being very high, makes the navigation dark. The Indians in going up this river travel as light as possible, to enable them to combat the strong current. The Hudson's Bay Company are supplied with a considerable quantity of peltry from this river.

As the description of this country, hitherto so little explored, is a principal part of what I intended in this publication, I have described it either from my own knowledge, or the most authentic information I was able to procure from the Savages. In this respect I have followed Carver, who on his arrival at the grand portage, met a large party of Killistinoe and Assinipoil Indians, from whom he received accounts of several lakes and rivers, which he describes agreeable to the information he obtained.

It is necessary to observe, that though the Indians are very expert in delineating countries upon bark, with wood coal mixed with bears' grease, and which even the women do with great precision, the length of a day's march is very uncertain, and consequently cannot afford any geographical information. This remark, I trust, will be found to want no farther proof than the consideration that their drafts consist principally of lakes and rivers, as they seldom travel much by land; and when their track over land is described, it is perhaps only a short portage which they cross, in order again to pursue their journey on their favourite element. But as few persons will probably read this account with a view of going into this country, the description I have been able to give will be sufficient for the generality of my readers. I lament exceedingly my inability to make this work more perfect, but trust that it will be found highly useful to those whose avocations may induce them to have recourse to it for information and guidance in commercial pursuits. If an Indian goes with the stream, or against it, from sun-rise to sun-set, it is called a day's march. This uncertainty makes it very difficult for any one who travels as a trader to ascertain any thing more than the Indian distance from one lake to another. As Mr. Carver, in his map, says that the branches which run from Riviére St. Louis, at the end of West Bay, in Lake Superior, are but little known, I can with equal propriety observe that those from Lake Alemipigon, or Nipegon, both east and west, are very difficult to describe geographically. The known candour of my countrymen, will, I am persuaded, pardon any errors of this sort, as I can assure them I have exerted my best endeavours to render the description of places, with respect to distances and situation, as clear as possible, which the chart I hope will more fully explain.

Further Transactions with the Indians; their Superstition, Jealousy, &c.

Having given an account of the different lakes, rivers, &c. from Lac la Mort, I shall continue the narrative from my return from Lake Manontoye, where I relieved Mr. Shaw.

A few days after, another band of Savages arrived with skins, furs, and some provisions; they stayed with me two days, making merry with what rum I could spare them, without doing any mischief, and departed at last very peaceably. On the twenty-third of February another band came in, consisting of about eighty, men, women, and children, who brought dried meats, oats, bears' grease, and eight packs of beaver, which I purchased, giving them rum, as usual, with which they got intoxicated. In this frolic one woman was killed, and a boy terribly burnt. On the third day they departed, well pleased with their reception, leaving us plenty of provisions. The weather being more moderate, I sent my men to the lake to look after the nets, which had been under the ice a considerable time, the severity of the season not having allowed us to examine them for near a month, when, to our great mortification they were found almost rotten, and not a single fish; but as one of the Canadians could make nets as well as myself, we repaired the damage, and caught plenty of fish to support us till April.

The severity of the season was sensibly felt by Mr. James Clark, belonging to the same company, who had five men starved at Lake Savan, a bad lake for fish, about three hundred and fifty miles from my wintering ground; the Indians being obliged to hunt so far back in the woods that they could not give him any assistance; and from the concurrent accounts of the traders in the north-west, as well as from the Savages who resorted to my house, it was the hardest winter they ever remembered.

About this time a large band of Chippeways arrived, traded with me for their hunt, and finished their frolic in a peaceable manner. While this band was with me, a curious circumstance occurred, which I shall relate.

One part of the religious superstition of the Savages, consists in each of them having his *totam*, or favourite spirit, which he believes watches over him. This *totam* they conceive assumes the shape of some beast or other, and therefore they never kill, hunt, or eat the animal whose form they think this *totam* bears.

The evening previous to the departure of the band, one of them, whose *totam* was a bear, dreamed that if he would go to a piece of swampy ground, at the foot of a high mountain, about five days march from my wigwaum, he would see a large herd of elks, moose, and other animals; but that he must be accompanied by at least ten good hunters. When he awoke he acquainted the band with his dream, and desired them to go with him: they all refused, saying it was out of their way, and that their hunting grounds were nearer. The Indian having a superstitious reverence for his dream (which ignorance, and the prevalence of example among the Savages, carries to a great height), thinking himself obliged to do so, as his companions had refused to go with him, went alone, and coming near the spot, saw the animals he dreamed of; he instantly fired, and killed a bear. Shocked at the transaction, and dreading the displeasure of the Master of Life, whom he conceived he had highly offended, he fell down, and lay senseless for some time: recovering from his state of insensibility, he got up, and was making the best of his way to my house, when he was met in the road by another large bear, who pulled him down, and scratched his face. The Indian relating this event at his return, added, in the simplicity of his nature, that the bear asked him what could induce him to kill his *totam*; to which he replied, that he did not know he was among the animals when he fired at the herd; that he was very sorry for the misfortune, and hoped he would have pity on him: that the bear suffered him to depart, told him to be more cautious in future, and acquaint all the Indians with the circumstance, that their *totams* might be safe, and the Master of Life not angry with them. As he entered my house, he looked at me very earnestly, and pronounced these words; " *Amik,* " *bunjey ta Kitchee Annascartissey nind, O Totam, cawwicha nee wee.* " *geossay sannegat debwoye :*"—or, " Beaver, my faith is lost, my " *totam* is angry, I shall never be able to hunt any more."

This idea of destiny, or, if I may be allowed the phrase, " *totamism,*" however strange, is not confined to the Savages; many instances might be adduced from history, to prove how strong these impressions have been on minds above the vulgar and unlearned. To instance one, in the history of the private life of Louis the XV. translated by Justamond, among some particulars of the life of the famous Samuel Bernard, the Jew banker, of the court of France, he says, that he was superstitious as the people of his nation are, and had a black hen, to which he thought his destiny was attached; he had the greatest care taken of her, and the loss of this fowl was, in fact, the period of his own existence, in January, 1739.

Dreams are particularly attended to by the Indians, and sometimes they make an artful use of the veneration that is paid to them, by which they carry a point they have in view: I shall relate an instance for the satisfaction of the reader.

Sir William Johnson, sitting in council with a party of Mohawks, the head chief told him, he had dreamed last night, that he had given him a fine laced coat, and he believed it was the same he then wore; Sir William smiled, and asked the chief if he really dreamed it; the Indian immediately answered in the affirmative: Well then, says Sir William, you must have it; and instantly pulled it off, and desiring the chief to strip himself, put on him the fine coat. The Indian was highly delighted, and when the council broke up, departed in great good humour, crying out, *wbo-ab!* which is an expression of great satisfaction among them.

The next council which was held, Sir William told the chief that he was not accustomed to dream, but that since he met him at the council, he had dreamed a very surprising dream; the Indian wished to know it; Sir William, with some hesitation, told him he had dreamed that he had given him a track of land on the Mohawk River to build a house on, and make a settlement, extending about nine miles in length along the banks: the chief smiled, and looking very cheerfully at Sir William, told him, if he really dreamed it he should have it; but that he would never dream again with him, for he had only got a laced coat, whereas Sir William was now entitled to a large bed, on which his ancestors had frequently slept. Sir William took possession of the land by virtue of an Indian deed signed by the chiefs, and gave them some rum to finish the business. It is now a considerable estate, but since the war the Americans have deprived him of it, with all the buildings, &c. which are very valuable. It lies on the opposite shore to the German Flats, but the land is by no means equal in goodness with the soil there. Perhaps no part of America produces land better calculated for cultivation than the German Flats.

During the American war, the best Loyalist troops were collected from the Mohawk River, and it was agreed on all hands that for steadiness, bravery and allegiance, they were not to be excelled. Government has done its utmost to reward many of them for their services, by giving them land in Canada and Nova Scotia; and to those whom poverty obliged to solicit them, implements of husbandry. They are now in a very flourishing state, and there is no doubt but they will prove valuable friends and supporters of Great Britain on any future emergency.

During the severe weather, I had a narrow escape from a contrivance of the Indian who was occasionally with me, and whom I employed in hunting, and making marten traps: this was occasioned by jealousy, on account of his wife, who was a pretty young *Squaw*, of the Rat nation, and whom he suspected of infidelity.

Being short of provisions, and having only one faithful Canadian in the house, except the Indian and his wife, I desired him to make a number of marten traps, and set them in two different roads, called a fork. Having finished about two hundred, and set them in the woods, baited with fish heads, which these animals are very fond of, he returned, and I gave him some rum for his trouble. Every day, for a considerable time, he went regularly to examine them, and when successful, was always rewarded to his sàtisfaction. Having been unfortunate several days, I charged him with doing other business, instead of examining the traps, to which he made no reply. I communicated my suspicions to my man, and desired him to watch the Savage. The next day the Canadian discovered him in the woods dressing some partridges: when he returned home in the evening he asked for rum, which I refused, telling him he did not deserve any. This answer displeased him; and looking earnestly at me, he replied, that I did not use him well; for though he had been unsuccessful with his traps, his trouble was the same; and that he generally found them out of order, which obliged him to set them right, and employed him the whole day. This excuse did not make any alteration in my conduct, and I told him the weather was too bad to get at any rum. He then began to imagine that I suspected him, and knew of his laziness, and immediately opened his mind, telling me very frankly that he was jealous of me; and that his reason for not going to examine the marten traps, was to prevent any communication between me and his wife, which, had he been far distant from home, might have been easily effected; and for this reason he kept near the house to watch her, knowing that she was fond of me; but that if I would give him some rum, to drive away the bad spirit from his heart, he would endeavour to forget the injury I had done him.

Judging it prudent to remove his suspicions, I gave him two gallons of rum, a carrot of tobacco, a shirt, a pair of leggons, a scalping knife, &c. and several articles to his wife. Having received the presents, he called her to drink with him, and thank the trader with a cheerful heart for his great kindness. When they were a little merry he began to sing, and I heard him repeat these words: " *Mornooch Amik hee* " *zargetoone mentimoyamish ;*" or, " I do not care though the Beaver " loves my wife." This did not please me, as I knew his jealousy would increase in proportion to the quantity of liquor he drank. However, I used the utmost precaution, securing his weapons to prevent his doing me any injury. His wife hearing him repeat the words so frequently, began to be angry, and pulled his hair and scratched his face. I thought this a favourable opportunity to express my dislike, and told him he was a fool to be jealous; that I gave him the rum to drive away the bad spirit, but it had a contrary effect; that I never wanted any thing of his wife but to make or mend snow shoes, and always paid her for her trouble. Yes, cries the wife, he is a fool, Beaver, and I will beat him; which she instantly did, and cut his head with a glass bottle. I then interfered, and parted them.

The moment I was gone, he began the old song, and continued singing till he was sober; when getting up, he came to me and said, " Bea-" ver, I have seen the bad spirit in my dream, who told me that the " trader had robbed me." Irritated at the expression, I told him his lips never spoke truth, and that he had no sense; and thinking it right to suppress this humour, beat him very severely. When he had recovered his reason, he said to me, " Beaver, you have sense, though you " have spotted my carcase." I then remonstrated with him on the great

folly of being jealous; but he was sullen, and made no reply. He then called his wife, but she being asleep did not hear him; he called a second time, and asked for his gun, tomahawk, and scalping knife; but not receiving any answer, he was very angry, and said to me, "Beaver, " I will throw away my body;" to which I did not think it prudent to make any reply. He then laid himself down on the ground, and called his wife a third time. She came to him, and observing displeasure in his countenance, told him not to be angry with the Beaver, for he was a great warrior, and always opened his heart to them. He ordered her to bring him a bark bowl full of water, and set it down carefully between the Beaver's legs. Whilst she was gone for the water, he said to me, " Come here, Beaver, and I will shew you that I have nothing sweet on " my lips, but will speak the truth." The wife returned and placed the bowl of water as her husband directed; when it had stood some time he said, " Beaver, put your finger in the water, and let it remain till I tell you to take it out." I obeyed him with the utmost cheerfulness, and in a few minutes, by his desire, withdrew it. He then said, " Bea-
" ver, you know that a husband is so called because he is the master of
" weakness, and for that reason he should protect his wife ; and at the
" same time, you, as a trader, should not injure me: but that I may not
" accuse you unjustly, I will try you by my own thoughts. Beaver,
" look at my wife, and look at the water, and tell me where you put
" your finger ; if you cannot tell, you have certainly robbed me." I then put in my finger again, and pointed out the place. " No;" said he, looking earnestly at me and his wife, " as you cannot be certain
" that it is the exact place where you first put in your finger, neither can
" I be certain that you have not robbed me ; though I as much believe
" it, as you do that the place you pointed out was the exact spot." I

confessed myself surprised at his disbelief; but not willing to incense him, I told him I was sorry he should imagine me capable of such wickedness as to be guilty of injuring him, for my mind was as calm as the water in an undisturbed state; and after giving him a few presents, sent them away, injoining him to use his wife well, as she was perfectly innocent. As they departed, he said to me smiling, " Beaver, you " must get somebody else to look after your marten traps."

Shrewd observation of the Indian.

Adultery among the northern Savages is generally punished in a summary way by the husband, who either beats his wife very severely, or bites off her nose. It is extremely dangerous for a trader to be suspected, for when the husband is intoxicated, his jealousy rises into madness; and revenge, whether the party suspected be innocent or guilty, is continually to be expected. When the mind of an Indian is once affected, his passion increases in proportion to the quantity of rum which he drinks, though he has the art to conceal it when he is sober. It is the baneful effects of rum which puts every jealous thought in motion, and then it knows no bounds, till intoxication completely overpowers him, or returning sobriety restores his lost reason.

Effects of Rum which we taught them to drink.

Early in the month of April, I received a letter from Monsieur Jaques Santeron at Lake Schabeechevan, in the same employ as myself, to inform me that he was tired of being a servant, and thinking his labours not sufficiently rewarded, had determined to make a grand *coup*, having a number of fine packs which he purposed selling to the Hudson's Bay Company: that he should leave his wintering ground next morning with four birch canoes, and would write further particulars on bark, which he should nail against one of the crooked trees at the foot of the Grand Rapid, in case I should be disposed to come that way, and concluded with great *gaieté de cœur*, wishing me and all my friends very well.

I was greatly surprised on receiving this unpleasant intelligence, and particularly as I had never heard of his integrity being impeached in the smallest degree; and I was disappointed, as I expected him to pass my wintering ground on his return to Pays Plat.

Conceiving it my duty to exert my best endeavours to prevent the loss of so much property to my employers, I engaged *Kesconeek* the chief, and twenty Savages, under promise of being satisfied for their trouble, to conduct me to the crooked trees. We went off with the utmost expedition, and in a few days arrived at the spot, where I saw the piece of bark, as he described, and the following words written with charcoal, " *Adieu, mon cher ami, je prends mon départ avec courage,* " *et j'attends une bonne vente pour ma pelleterie. De bon cœur je vous* " *souhaite la prosperité ; faites mes compliments à tous mes amis—au re-* " *voir mon cher companion.*"

Having perused it, and explained it to the chief; he said he was a bad spirit, and that as he had been gone six days before our arrival, it would be impossible to overtake him, as he could not be far from the entrance of the North River, leading to Hudson's Bay, and if I pursued him, I should not get back in time to trade with the Indians for their great hunt. We therefore returned, after a fruitless expedition, extremely mortified at the disappointment, as I was very sensible he would never return to Canada, to make satisfaction to his employers.

Soon after my return the grand band came in with all their winter's hunt, which they call *Kitchee Artawway*. They consisted of about thirty families, of twenty in each. He who has most wives is considered the best hunter, being obliged to provide for their maintenance by his own industry. The Indians laugh at the Europeans for having only one wife, and that for life, as they conceive the good spirit formed them to be happy, and not to continue together unless their tempers and dispositions were congenial.

Having bartered for their skins and furs, they asked for rum; I told them I had only one small keg left, which I would give them at their departure, which satisfied them: and when they were ready to embark, I ordered a Canadian to put it into the chief's canoe.

Having disposed of all my merchandise except a few articles, and a small quantity of rum, to barter with any Indians I might happen to meet with in my return to Pays Plat, we baled up our peltry, and on the 23d of May left Lac la Mort, with four small birch canoes richly laden with the skins of beavers, otters, martens, minx, loup serviers, beaver eaters, foxes, bears, &c.

Before I proceed to relate the particulars of my voyage, I shall mention the Indian manner of killing the white bear and the buffalo. The large white bear, commonly called the grisly bear, is a very dangerous animal; when the Indians hunt it they generally go six or eight in a band; the instant they see one, they endeavour to surround it, by forming a large circle: if it is on the march they fire at it;—but it is most frequently discovered in the winter season sucking its paws; in that case they approach nearer, and form a double row for the animal to run between. One of the party is then sent out, who fires at the bear and generally wounds it: this rouzes it to pursue the Indian, who runs between the ranks, and the rest of the band fire and soon dispatch it.

The buffalo I need not describe; it is well known to be a remarkably strong animal; the Indians say its head is bullet proof, and therefore they always fire at the body, endeavouring to hit the heart. When they are in pursuit of this animal they make up small huts of snow in different places, for near a mile in length on each side of the road; in each of these huts an Indian stands with a bow and arrow, to shoot at it as it passes, preferring that mode to powder and ball, as it does not alarm the rest of the herd. The snow prevents the buffalo from smelling the Indians, though their scent is very strong and quick. The instant the animal drops they tomahawk it.

On the 2d of July we arrived at Portage Plain, so called on account of its being a barren rock, near a mile long, joining to Lake Alemipigon: it was sun-set when we encamped. Besides the sixteen Canadians, our party was increased considerably by about twenty of the Sturgeon and Nipegon Indians, who accompanied us according to the usual custom of following the trader to assist at the carrying places. The day previous to our departure some traders overtook us, and encamped also. They informed us of a band of Indians who were enemies to the Nipegons being near at hand, and desired me to acquaint the Savages with it. Before their arrival the Sturgeon Indians left us, and the other band would fain have quitted the ground; but upon telling them I wanted their assistance on my journey, they agreed to stay, though I thought very reluctantly.

We soon discovered several canoes, and in about half an hour the Indians landed. They were of the nation of the Wasses, and always at war with our Savages. Being a select people, they seldom associate with other tribes, and are continually on the hunt, only making their appearance in spring and autumn. We received them very cordially, and after the usual forms of salutation, made mutual presents to each other: they told me they had heard of me by some Indians at Lac la Mort, and were desirous of seeing me before my return to Michillimakinac, or in their language *Tecodondoragbie.*

I soon perceived the uneasiness of my Indians, and was careful to keep them at some distance from each other; but all my precaution was ineffectual, and before my departure a most dreadful catastrophe was the consequence of their mutual hatred.

Our Indians having made up huts, began to sing their medicine songs to induce the Wasses to partake of a feast which they said they intended to make, with a view of preventing any dispute with them; but knowing that the Nipegons had no provisions but what I found them, I suspected their intentions were not so pacific as they pretended: this induced me to ask a boy belonging to the band, why they pretended to make a feast, without having any provision to do it; he replied, that the Wasses had made them a present of dried meat, and with this and some huckle berries they had saved, they intended to make their visitants merry. This answer confirmed my suspicions, as no feast is ever made, where friendship is intended, without inviting the trader; and as no notice was sent me, I dreaded the evil consequence of their meeting.

Deliberating with myself on the unpleasant prospect, and considering how to act to prevent mischief, I was interrupted in my meditations by a Savage (*Ayarbee*, or the big man), who came to give me intelligence of an intended plan to destroy the Nipegon Indians, and which was communicated to him by an old woman who belonged to the band of Wasses.

In about an hour the Nipegon huts were in order to receive their intended guests, who were encamped in a hollow, surrounded with cedar trees and bushes, close to the lake side. The Nipegons being determined to counteract the designs of their deceitful visitors, and punish their intended perfidy, made holes in the bark of their huts, in which they placed their guns, loaded with swan shot. Each man taking his station; the Wasses, to the number of eighteen, ascended the hill, and were coming prepared to partake of the feast, with knives and wooden bowls, intending to overpower the Nipegons on a given signal; but they were fatally disappointed, for when they got within thirty yards of the Nipegon huts, they were fired at, and all the band, except a girl about fourteen years of age, killed on the spot; she was dangerously wounded, but advanced with a gun, which she snatched from an Indian who was preparing to dispatch her, and shot *Ayarbee* through the head, and was herself soon after tomahawked and scalped by a Nipegon boy about the same age, who at such an early period of life displayed all that ferocity which marks the most determined chief.

Thus was treachery rewarded: and though in my heart I could not but approve of the conduct of the Nipegon Indians, I was afraid of trusting to them, and had resolved on taking my leave of them, when the chief came up and informed me, he was very sorry that his band could not accompany me any farther, for being afraid of the resentment of the nation of the Wasses, when they came to hear of the transaction, notwithstanding they had done it in their own defence, they had determined to depart; and soon after pushed off their canoes, and left me, a circumstance which pleased me exceedingly. The next day a party of Indians met us, to whom I related the disaster. They were very much shocked, and said the Nipegon Savages might repent their rash conduct, though at the same time they acknowledged them right in guarding against the designs of the Wasses. They asked me if I had got their packs, as they assured me they had made a good hunt, and had rich peltry. This information vexed me exceedingly, as I should certainly have increased my cargo had not the affair happened, and likewise have given more satisfaction to my employers, though I had already a large quantity of goods, and had every reason to be pleased with my success. The Nipegons made up fourteen bales of dried meat, which they took with them; but the furs and skins were hidden in the woods, and never afterwards found that I heard of.

We continued our journey to Lac Eturgeon, where soon after our landing, we killed a great many wild fowl, and caught plenty of fish. Here we met about fifty of the Hawoyzask or Rat Nation Indians, with whom I made a small barter, chiefly with rum, having disposed of all my Indian goods.

Our journey was retarded for some time in order to gratify my curiosity. A young Indian girl fell sick, and the chief desired me to stay to see the wonderful effects of their medicines, as she was very bad, and without immediate assistance, he said, must soon change her climate. The physician who attended her said, that the *Matchee Mannitoo*, or bad spirit, had put the bear's claws into her, and his medicines would remove them. A hut was prepared, and the girl stripped to her *matcheecoaty* or under petticoat; she was then painted with vermilion, and daubed over with soot and bears' grease, and profusely sweated, which soon relieved her pain. During the operation, the physician addressed himself to the Master of Life, begging his assistance, and thanking him for giving knowledge to restore health: then giving her a decoction of roots, he made a perfect cure. I could not help admiring his skill and manner of proceeding, though I attributed her recovery solely to the plentiful perspiration she underwent.

Previous to our departure, one of their women was delivered of a fine boy, and I was highly delighted with the mother's tenderness, as the infant sucked the milk, which in their language is called *tootoosbonarbo*, or the sap of the human breast, an expression which struck me forcibly. The husband was also very attentive, and performed the part of an affectionate parent, which induced me to give him some rum to cheer his heart, and drink my health. He seemed pleased with the present, and addressing himself to the Great Spirit, thanked him for the safe delivery of his *mentimoye*:—then looking very earnestly at me, told me how much he was indebted to me for the comfort that I had afforded him, and that he was sure that I was a brave warrior, for my generosity to him and his wife, when they so much wanted assistance. When the young warrior cried, he observed, that he wished to be grateful to me for my attention to his parents, and that it was only the echo of his breath, (meaning his voice) to praise the goodness of the *Saggonasb*, or Englishman. As I got into my canoe, he said, " Beaver, be strong, you will always " have a public road among the Nipegon Indians, therefore return as " soon as you can; in the mean time, I shall take care to acquaint all " the Indians with your goodness, and I hope when we see you again, " we shall have had a good hunt, and be able to give you furs and skins " to repay your kindness." I told him I always loved the Indians, that I was adopted by the Chippeways, and considered myself as one of their tribe; that I would return as soon as possible with plenty of goods for their families; that my heart was melted by his regard for me, and giving him and his wife each a parting glass of the strong water, took my leave, and pursued my journey.

We arrived at Pays Plat on the 10th of August, where I met some brother traders, who had been in different parts of the inlands, particularly the North-west. Here we waited for fresh goods from our employers, and enjoyed ourselves with the remains of our different provisions, which we threw into a common stock, and made ourselves merry with the scanty pittance, recounting our several adventures: but none of them had suffered the difficulties I had experienced, except Mr. Shaw, whom I happily relieved at Lake Manontoye; the rest of the traders having wintered very remote from me, by the way of the Grand Portage.

Soon after our arrival, our employers sent their agents with a fresh assortment of merchandize and provisions, which rejoiced us exceedingly, having been a considerable time without corn or grease, and absent from Michillimakinac about fourteen months. I delivered my cargo of furs, consisting of about one hundred and forty packs, in good condition, and loaded the canoes with the fresh goods; then taking leave of my companions, prepared for my departure for the Inlands, to winter another year among the Nipegon Savages. But before I begin to relate my second adventure, I cannot forbear making some observations on the hardships attending an Indian life, particularly as an interpreter and trader.

My salary was about one hundred and fifty pounds per annum, which I certainly deserved, considering the knowledge I had of the Chippeway language.

I was sent into the Inlands with only corn and hard grease, without any other provisions I could rely on; for as to fish and other animal food, the former in a great measure depends on the season, the latter on the arrival of Savages; and though in general I was successful in aquatic pursuits, and received frequent supplies from the Indians, it was a precarious mode of subsistence, and at Lac la Mort I suffered great hardships.

I had sixteen men, and an Indian and his wife occasionally with me, to feed and govern, and on the continuance of their health my existence in a great measure depended. As it was my constant duty to be in the way, in case of the arrival of Savages, being the only one who could talk their language, I had few opportunities of hunting, neither could I go far abroad to examine whether the Canadians did their duty or not: I was therefore always full of anxiety, and rejoiced when the spring returned to set me free.

The constant attention necessary in taking care of the goods to prevent depredations, the continual fears and apprehensions of being plundered by a set of intoxicated beings; always liable to insults, without daring to resent them; and when I had bartered all my merchandize, and made a successful trip—feeling a painful solicitude till the fruits of my labours were safely delivered to my employers. Upon the whole, perhaps no situation can be more distressing, and it has often filled my mind with surprise when I reflected on the engagement I entered into, which consumed the prime of my days in a traffic, the dangers and fatigues of which scarce any salary could compensate. I believe nothing but the flattering idea of thinking myself superior to others as an interpreter, prompted me to continue in a station so fatiguing to support, and so difficult to execute; and I cannot but conclude with this observation :—That however censurable a man may be for indulging even this degree of pride, the liberal mind will easily pardon the presumption, as they know he alone is the sufferer; and as self-opinion governs the pursuits of mankind, the individual who is most influenced by it, must stand or fall by the consequences.

SECOND EXPEDITION.

Proceed to winter again among the Nipegon Indians;—Design of an Indian to plunder us;—unfortunate Accident happens to an Indian Chief;—narrowly escape being assassinated by an Indian Straggler; Murder of Joseph la Forme, a Trader.

On the 15th of August I left Pays Plat, with four birch canoes, and the same men who wintered with me at Lac la Mort, and arrived at Riviére la Pique, which runs into Lake Superior: this river is very crooked for about seven miles, and extremely deep; it abounds with fish, particularly pike, from which it takes its name. On our landing, we found a large band of Chippeways, and some of the Rat nation, who immediately prepared a feast for us of dried meat, fish, &c. Among them was an Indian named *Ogasby,* or the horse; he was reckoned, even by his own tribe, a bad Indian, which put me on my guard during my encampment there. I traded for their skins and furs, and gave them some rum, with which they had a frolic, which lasted for three days and nights; on this occasion five men were killed, and one woman dreadfully burnt. When the fumes of the liquor had evaporated, they began, as usual, to reflect on the folly of their conduct, and all except *Ogasby* expressed great concern; he seemed rather to be pleased at the mischief which had happened, and before my departure, I was informed that he intended to destroy me, and plunder the property. To frustrate his villainous intention, I kept him in good humour, and made him sleep in my hut, a compliment he seemed highly pleased with, and which I believe for the time diverted him from his purpose; and though by no means fond of his company, I judged it most prudent to have my enemy in sight. In the morning I gave him a glass of rum, and promised him a two-gallon keg to carry off the ground, which, as the Indians express themselves, drove the bad spirit from his heart. When my men had prepared every thing for embarkation, I gave the chief of the band the liquor, and a single bottle of rum more than I promised to *Ogasby*, unknown to the rest, in which I had infused a considerable quantity of laudanum. Unsuspicious of what I had done, he put the bottle to his mouth, and shaking me by the hand, said to me, "*Kee ta-linimanco negee*," or, " your health, friend," and immediately took a hearty draught which soon stupified and lulled him into a profound sleep, in which, I was afterwards informed, he remained twelve hours, depriving him of the power of doing harm, and that soon after, an Indian who had an antipathy against him, and only sought an opportunity of gratifying his resentment, tomahawked him. His eldest son burnt him, and fixed his bones on a high pole, as he was the head chief of the tribe.

We proceeded on our voyage, and arrived at a short carrying place, called Portage la Rame, where we encamped for nine days, being wind bound; here we found a number of Indians in the same situation.

As soon as Lake Superior was passable with safety, we continued our journey through strong and dangerous rapids, which kept us continually in the water, and very sensibly affected our limbs; on these occasions,

P

where great exertion is necessary, all distinction is laid aside, and it is *tel maître, tel valet*, the bourgeois must work as hard as the engagés, to encourage them to do their duty with more alacrity, and avoid all cause of complaint.

The wind proving favourable, we proceeded to Cranberry Lake, so called from the great quantity of cranberries growing in the swamps. We stopped here two days to refresh ourselves after the great fatigue we had undergone in struggling against the rapids. Being sufficiently recovered, and having nothing to detain us, we proceeded to a short carrying place called *La grande Côte de la Roche*, at the entrance of the Nipegon River, which is a high ridge of rocks that must be passed to avoid the great cataract which I mentioned in my former voyage. At this time we had very little animal food, but fortunately killed three large bears in the middle of the portage, which supported us several days, besides which, we reserved some of the meat we had smoked and dried to carry with us.

From *La grande Côte de la Roche* we proceeded to *Lac le Nid au Corbeau*, or Crow's Nest Lake, which is about two hundred miles in circumference, and supplied by a number of small rivers; there are also several islands on it which furnish the Indians with great plenty of wild fowl: bears are also found here in abundance, and a surprising number of beaver dams, running in a crooked direction about ten miles. The Chippeways hunt here, and find a great deal of game.

The reader will observe that in the first voyage I gave an account of another Crow's Nest Lake, which is very small, with an island in the middle with high palm trees : in such an extent of country it is not surprising that there should be two places of the same name.

During our stay a band of Indians arrived from Lake Arbitibis, who probably were dissatisfied with the trader they dealt with, and intended to go to Michillimakinac, but finding that I understood their language, they bartered with me, and made me a present of meat and fish. An accident happened here which had nearly proved fatal, and which was of infinite service to me ever after, by putting me more on my guard in all transactions with the Savages.

Some of the chiefs being desirous of seeing my North-west guns, I was obliged to open a case for their inspection; this I did unwillingly, as the weather was fine, and I was extremely anxious to get to the wintering ground before a heavy fall of snow : having shewn them the guns, they loaded four, and laid them down by the cases, intending to try them ; during the time they were thus employed I was busy in arranging the goods that had been displaced in getting at them; but as soon as I was at leisure, I took up one of the guns in a careless manner, not knowing it was charged, and snapped the lock, which most unfortunately shot off the ear of one of the chiefs, and I also received some injury by the powder flying in my face, and almost depriving me of sight. The discharge was so instantaneous, and appeared so premeditated that the chief reproached me in very severe terms for the injury I had done him, and threatened revenge ; however, I soon convinced him it was an accident, and giving him some presents, he consoled himself for the loss of his ear, which was very large and handsome, and without a single break, which made it very valuable in his estimation. It was for-

tunate I did not kill him, as in all probability we should have been
sacrificed to the resentment of the band.

The Indians pride themselves in having large ears, and extended as
wide as possible, which renders them liable to be pulled off. It is very
common in drunken frolics to lose them; but when they are only torn,
they cut them smooth with a knife, and sew the parts together with a
needle and deers' sinews, and after sweating in a stove, resume their
usual cheerfulness.

The next day we took our leave, and pursued our journey to *She-
carke Sakiegan*, or the Shunk's Lake, which runs with a strong current.
In the fall it abounds with geese and ducks: here we hunted one day,
and with good success. The next morning at break of day we embarked, and had favourable weather till we arrived at Lake Schabeechevan, or the Weed Lake. This lake is about one hundred and
eighty miles in circumference, and full of small islands; it abounds
with fish, and the swamps are full of wild rice and cranberries; it is
about six days march from Lac la Mort.

This lake was an unfortunate situation to my employers last year,
when one of their servants, Jaques Santeron, went off with a valuable
cargo. On my arrival, I looked out for the house he had erected, but
could not discern the least trace of it; probably he was so elated that
he made a *feu de joye* on the prospect of being his own master. At the
extremity of this lake is a fall of water, which runs from a river of the
same name, and has a direct communication with the waters leading
from Fort Albany, within the boundaries of the Hudson's Bay territo-

ries: it is about thirty days march across nineteen portages and creeks, besides fourteen rapids, which are a great hindrance to the journey. The Indians run down the strong currents without the least fear, and seldom meet with any accident, performing the voyage in one third part of the time they take in ascending, and without any damage to their canoes, which in going against the stream are frequently rendered useless, and they are obliged to make new ones, before they can pursue their voyage; but it is a most convenient circumstance that they are no where at a loss for birch bark, and being also very expert, they will make a canoe in three days sufficiently large to carry three people with necessaries for their support, and room to stow their furs and skins. On this lake there are about one hundred and fifty good hunters, who make a great many packs of beaver, &c. and this was one inducement for settling here, which was increased by the prospect of a plentiful supply of fish, rice, and cranberries, which are winter comforts of too great consequence to be slighted.

Having secured the canoes, and refreshed my men with good soup, I left them in charge of the goods, and took two Indians to shew me a convenient place to build a house, which having fixed on, a building was erected, fifty feet long, and twenty feet wide, divided into two separate apartments, one for merchandise, and the other for common use. The rum being concealed in the woods, and every thing properly arranged, we put the fishing tackle in order; and as the lakes began to freeze very fast, I divided my men into two parties, one half to be employed in fishing, the remainder (except one man whom I always kept in the house) in providing fuel for winter. In about three weeks a sufficient quantity of wood was piled near the house, and the wood cutters joined the fishing party: they proved very successful, so that our minds were more at ease than in the preceding year, not having the dread of famine.

In about ten days a numerous band of Indians arrived with their fall hunt, none of whom I had ever seen, not having wintered so far inland before. They seemed well pleased to find a trader settled among them, and particularly as I spoke the language; but when I informed them that I was a brother warrior, and shewed the marks of adoption in my flesh, they were highly delighted. The women were immediately ordered to make up huts, and prepare a feast; whilst this was doing the Indians came into my house, one by one, and seating themselves on the floor, began to smoke, and looked very cheerful. When I had given them tobacco and other Indian goods, the old chief, whose name was *Mattoyash,* or the Earth, took me round the neck, and kissed my cheek, then addressed me in the following words.

" *Meegwoitch kitchee mannitoo, kaygait kee zargetoone an Nishin-*
" *norbay nogome, shashyyar paysbik artawway winnin tercushenan, caw-*
" *ween kitchee morgussey, an Nishinnorbay nogome cawwickar inde-*
" *nendum. Kaygait kitchee mushkowway geosay baguarmissey way-*
" *benan matchee oathty nee zargetoone Saggonash artawway; winnin*
" *kaygait hapadgey kitchee morgussey an Nishinnorbay; kaygwotch*
" *annaboycassey neennerwind mornooch towwarch nee zargey deb-*
" *woye kee appay omar, cuppar behoue nepewar appiminiqui omar.*"—
" I thank the Master of Life for loving us Indians, and sending us this
" day an English trader, who will open his heart to me and my young
" men. Take courage, young men, suffer not your hearts to be bound

VOYAGES AND TRAVELS. 111

" up, and throw away the bad spirit from you: we all love the English
" traders, for we have heard of their pity to Savages; we believe that
" they have an open heart, that their veins run clear like the sun. It
" is true we Indians have but little sense when drunk, but we hope
" you will not think of this, and if you will stay with us, we will hunt
" with spirit for you."

When he had finished his speech they all got up, and taking me by
the right hand, conducted me to their hut; immediately on entering, one
of the warriors placed me on a large beaver robe which was prepared
for me, and put a wampum belt round my neck, singing all the time to
the Master of Life, while myself and the chief were eating. When the
feast was over, I took two of the Indians to my house, and gave them
two kegs of rum, and ten carrots of tobacco, with other articles, for
which they gave me all their peltry. They then began to frolic, which
continued three days and nights: the only accident which happened was
to a little child, whose back was broke by the mother. When they had
rested a day after intoxication, I supplied them with plenty of ammunition for their winter's hunt, and they departed perfectly satisfied with
their reception. I cannot help relating the method I was obliged to
adopt to quiet an old Indian woman, who was more troublesome than
the rest, and continually importuned me for liquor.

I infused forty drops of the tincture of cantharides, and the same
quantity of laudanum, into a glass of rum, and when she came to me
soliciting very earnestly for the strong water, I gave her the dose which
was prepared for her: she drank it without hesitation, and being already
much intoxicated, it made her stagger. But this did not satisfy her, and

she still asked for more; I then repeated the dose, which she also drank, and then fell on the floor. I ordered my Canadian to carry her out of the house, and lay her carefully near her own wigwaum, where she remained twelve hours in a deep sleep, to my entire satisfaction. I have always found laudanum extremely useful; in general it may be considered an essential article in the commerce with the Indians, as it proves the only method of overcoming their intoxicated senses, and making the life of a trader more tolerable, by putting a stop to their impertinence.

On the 19th of November a band of about forty Indians came in with a few skins and a great quantity of dried meat, with some bears' grease, which I purchased for a little rum, and advised them to carry it along with them off the ground; they complied with my wishes, and embarked perfectly sober.

It was always my custom to endeavour to persuade them to take away the rum, though I seldom succeeded. The fatigue of watching them when the liquor begins to operate is inconceivable, besides the risk of our lives and property.

After their departure I was left for near a month with only one man, the rest being employed in fishing and watching the marten traps: in both pursuits they were successful, but particularly in the former, having brought home near eight thousand, trout, pike, pickerill, and white fish, which we hung up as usual to freeze. When the severe weather sets in every man has his allowance served out twice a day, and this rule is constantly adhered to even though the stock be very considerable.

VOYAGES AND TRAVELS.   113

In the beginning of December a new married couple arrived, and having given them a little rum, they got very merry; and perceiving the woman was in great good humour, I desired her to sing a love-song, which she consented to with cheerfulness.

THE SONG.

" *Debwoye, nee zargay ween aighter, paysbih oathty, seizeebockquoit
" shenargussey me tarbiscoach nepeech cassawicha nepoo, moszack pe-
" martus, seizeebockquoit meteek.*"

" It is true I love him only whose heart is like the sweet sap that
" runs from the sugar-tree, and is brother to the aspin leaf, that al-
" ways lives and shivers."

I thanked her for her song, and giving the husband a bottle of *scuttaywabo*, left them together to enjoy their hearts' delight; and as there was not sufficient to intoxicate them, I was not afraid of a jealous fit. I always bore in mind the circumstance at Lac la Mort, and my fortunate escape. In the morning they departed, paying me well for my presents with some beaver, bear, and otter skins.

A few days after an Indian arrived, with his two wives and three children; they immediately came into my house, and sat down by the fire. I thought I discovered deceit in his countenance, and watched him very narrowly. I asked him what success he had met with in his hunt? He told me he believed the Master of Life was angry with him, for he had fired at several animals, and expended all his ammunition, without doing execution. This was a figurative mode of expression,

Q

and convinced me that he was lazy, and could not get credit for what he wanted: he added, that his family had been without provisions some days, and hoped I would cheer their hearts, and be a friend to them. I then ordered a large kettle to be put on the fire, and boiled some fish, which they ate of very heartily, particularly the women and children.

I questioned him concerning his hunting grounds: he told me he was from Hudson's Bay, and had come so far, hearing some traders were settled at Shunk's Lake, and as he knew there were plenty of animals, he expected to get a great many skins. This I was convinced was false, and I immediately considered him as a straggler, or he certainly would not have travelled so far, unless he had done something to displease the servants at the Company's forts, and could not obtain credit. Looking at me very earnestly, he asked me to trust him a gun, blanket, and ammunition; but I refused him: this displeased him; and going out of the house, one of them called him, the other followed him out, and said something to him in a low tone of voice: this appeared to me like a confederacy, and put me on my guard. In a few minutes he returned, and renewed his solicitations; saying, " Are you " afraid to trust me forty skins? I will pay you in the spring."— I told him I never gave credit to any but good hunters, and I was sure he was an idle straggler, who lived without industry, and advised him to return to his own tribe, and solicit their assistance who knew him better than I did. So severe a check to his application (and which I was afterwards sorry for) seemed to rouze the bad spirit in his heart, and he left me under the influence of the *Matebee. Mannitoo*, and went down to his canoe, seeming to be in deep discourse with his wives.

My man observing them, watched them very narrowly, and saw the Indian endeavouring to file off the end of his gun, to make it convenient to conceal under his blanket; having shortened and loaded it, he returned with it hid under his dress. This transaction being a convincing proof of his diabolical intention, I directed my man to stand on one side of the door, and I took my post on the other, waiting his entrance into the house. Just as he passed the threshold, I knocked him down with a billet of wood, and taking his short gun from him, beat him so much that we were obliged to carry him down to his canoe, where his family were waiting for him, and ordered them all off the ground, threatening that in case of refusal his canoe should be instantly broken to pieces, and his family turned adrift. The squaws and children appeared very much distressed, and with great reluctance obeyed my orders. Thus I got rid of an unprincipled set; and, as will soon appear, escaped a danger which was certainly intended to involve me and my men in utter ruin.

A few days after their departure, an Indian arrived and informed me that Mr. Joseph la Forme, a brother trader who was settled at Lac le Sel, was killed by a Savage, and described his person. I had no doubt but he was the same man who attempted to destroy me. I communicated every circumstance of his conduct, and the revenge I took on the occasion. The Indian congratulated me on my happy escape, as he was known to be a bad man by all the tribe, having killed his brother and one of his wives last fall, which was the reason that the band he belonged to would not suffer him to stay among them. As I was anxious to know the particulars, I desired him to relate them. He told me that he was informed by a Savage whom he accidentally met, and to whom the murderer had revealed the particulars, that the Indian being disappointed in his design against me, pursued his journey with the bad spirit in his heart, and arrived at Joseph La Forme's house, which he entered, and asked for rum and tobacco, which was given him; but observing he had not any thing to trade with, La Forme was suspicious of him: whilst he was smoking he asked for credit, but was refused, and told that he was not only a bad hunter, but that he had a heart of lead. This imprudent reproach incensed him, and observing no one in the house but the trader, (the men being fishing) he watched a convenient opportunity, and when La Forme stooped to light his pipe, shot him through the head, plundered the house of a few things, and went off.

On this information I dispatched six Indians, with a trusty Canadian, to endeavour to secure the property, in which they fortunately succeeded, and brought away all the peltry, merchandise, &c. and the deceased trader's men, whom I engaged in my service. About six weeks after, one of the tribe whom he had formerly offended, and who had heard of this recent act of villainy, after repeated reproaches for his baseness, tomahawked him, cut off his head, and brought it to my house to shew my Indians.

The unhappy fate of Joseph La Forme affords a melancholy example of the precarious situation of all Indian traders; and furnishes a useful lesson of instruction to those who may in future be engaged in commerce with the Savages—that it is frequently more prudent to conceal resentment than to gratify it.

We are reduced to great Hardships for want of Provisions;—relieved by the fortunate Arrival of some Indians.—Narrative of a most shocking Transaction perpetrated by one Janvier, belonging to a Mr. Fulton, a Trader—Mr. Fulton takes Means to induce a Confession, and punishes him accordingly.—Visit from a Trader belonging to the Hudson's Bay Company—some Observations concerning that Trade, and the Conduct of the Company towards their Servants.

THE latter end of January, 1779, a band of the Rat Nation arrived, belonging to *Sheharhistergoan*, or the Skunk's-head Lake, which is between Lake Nipegon and Lake Manontoye. They brought me provisions and furs, which I bartered for; giving them rum, as usual, of which they drank freely without doing any mischief. After their departure we were short of provisions, having a larger household to provide for, by taking La Forme's men into my service. We were reduced to a few fish and some wild rice, or *menomon* (which are kept in *muccucks*, or bark boxes), to support myself and seventeen men; the allowance to each being only a handful of rice and a small fish, about 2lb. weight, which is boiled together and makes pleasant soup. I have often been surprised that fish-broth is not more generally used, as it is certainly very palatable; but I am not sufficiently informed in medical knowledge to speak either of its wholesomeness or nutritive qualities. Sturgeon broth is delicious, and leaves a pleasing taste on the tongue; but as it rather increases the appetite for food, as I have experienced, it should not be taken but when there is plenty of meat to be got. This fish is very common in Albany, and is sold at 1d. per lb. York currency. The flesh is called Albany beef.

The frost continuing very severe, and no appearance of Indians to supply our wants, we were obliged to take off the hair from the bear skins, and roast the hide, which tastes like pork. This, with some *tripe de roche* boiled, was all our nourishment.

Tripe de roche, or *hawercoon*, is a weed that grows to the rocks, of a spongy nature, and very unwholesome, causing violent pains in the bowels, and frequently occasions a flux. I am informed the traders in the North-west, have often experienced this disorder; and some of them, in very severe weather, have been compelled to eat it for fourteen days successively, which weakened them exceedingly. When the disorder does not terminate in a flux, it occasions a violent vomiting, and sometimes spitting of blood, with acute spasms in the bowels.

After suffering great hardships, I advised my men to make marten traps, and set them in the woods as they did last winter at Lac la Mort, which supplied us occasionally, but very short of our real wants. At last a band of Indians arrived with ten slay load of meat and furs, which relieved us, and gave us fresh spirits. My men discovered them at a distance, and, though much enfeebled by severe hunger, put on their snow-shoes to meet them.

It is surprising what efforts nature makes to support distress, and how cheerfully she struggles when the prospect of relief is near at hand; every painful recollection of past sufferings quickly vanishes, and new life seems to breathe through every vein. Those who live in constant luxury, and are ignorant of the meaning of the bread of carefulness, are strangers to the joy arising from an unexpected supply, and sitting down to a table in the wilderness. Hunger needs not the borrowed aid of sauce; and, in the language of Pope, " To enjoy, is to obey."—How delightful is such obedience!

The Indians seeing our distress by our looks, which were very meagre, gave us all their provisions, consisting of bear, racoon, and moose. The kettle was soon put on the fire, and we made a comfortable repast, with cheerful hearts; the Indians during the time enjoying the happiness of relieving our wants.

Notwithstanding the cruelty of Savages, they possess virtues which do honour to human nature, and exhibit instances of generosity and kindness which the most philanthropic soul cannot exceed. They are ignorant of those mean sordid sentiments which disgrace many more enlightened, and more wealthy; and from the knowledge I have of their disposition, I am sure they would blush at the parsimonious conduct of those whom Providence hath blessed with affluence.

After the repast, the chief (not willing to disturb us before) asked for some tobacco, and having smoked some time, said he had bad news to tell me, which some Indians had informed him of, concerning Mr. Fulton, then at *Shekarkistergoan*, and which he was sorry to relate, as it affected him exceedingly. I desired him to finish his pipe, and drink a glass of rum before he began the story; and at the same time mentioned my surprise at not hearing of any remarkable circumstance, having traded with a band of the Rat nation within a few days, who came from that Lake. He told me he had met the band, and related the affair to them, who were much astonished; but as Mr. Fulton's men were not returned from fishing when they left the place, the transaction was not known till after their departure.

Mr. Fulton being obliged to divide his men into two parties, which is called the *cawway*, or casting lots, which party shall hunt and fish, and which shall stay with the master, did so accordingly. The fishing party consisted of Charles Janvier, François St. Ange, and Lewis Dufresne, all natives of Canada, who, being provided with axes, ice-cutters, and fishing materials, set off, and at the expiration of eight days arrived at a convenient place, where they built a hut, in which they lived for some time tolerably well; but fish failing them, and having no success in hunting, they were almost starved. In this situation, said the chief, the bad spirit had entered into the heart of Janvier, and he being the strongest man, supported hunger better than his companions, by which he was enabled soon after to effect a diabolical purpose he had formed, of killing the first Indian who should come in his way, and which he had declared he would do. In the height of their distress Janvier perceived a Savage at some distance, with a load at his back, and instantly returning to the hut, told his poor dispirited partners of their approaching relief. They instantly got up, though very weak, and came out of the hut as fast as their feeble limbs would allow them. The Indian arrived, took off his load, which was only two otters, and two hares, and gave them to Janvier, who received them with great satisfaction; and when he had skinned them, boiled them in the kettle without cleansing them, so extreme was their hunger. This seasonable relief was soon devoured, and from the eagerness with which Janvier eat, and the satisfaction which appeared in his countenance when he looked at the Savage, the men were in hopes he had forgot the rash determination he had formed, and flattered themselves his mind was not so depraved as to entertain a thought of doing an injury to the man whose timely assistance had saved their lives. The next morning the Indian told them he was sorry he could not assist them further, having no ammunition, but that he was going to Mr. Fulton for a supply.

Janvier's heart being inexorable even to the kindness he had received, he desired the Savage to assist him in placing a large log of wood on the fire, as his companions were unable to do it. The Indian cheerfully complied, and stooping to take it up, Janvier knocked him down with an axe and dragged him to the door of the hut, cut him up, and with the most unfeeling barbarity put as much of the flesh of his deliverer into the kettle as he thought sufficient for a meal. When it was dressed, he compelled François St. Ange, and Louis Dufresne, to partake of it, and obliged them to kiss the cross which hung at his breast, and swear by all the saints never to reveal the transaction; threatening, at the same time, that if they did they should share the same fate. Intimidated by his threats, and the certainty that he would fulfil them, they solemnly promised perfect compliance with his injunctions. Having overcome their first aversion, which extreme hunger had occasioned, they ate immoderately of the horrid meal, and soon after fell sick, with violent reachings. During their indisposition they complained to each other softly, that it was eating the Indian's flesh

[Here we find a genuine Savage from Europe —]

which had occasioned their sickness: Janvier overhearing them, called them fools and rascals, and asked them if they were afraid the Savage would come to life again; and with an insolent sneer desired them to tell him which they thought the best part of a man? The poor fellows only replied they were very sick and could not tell the cause. In a few days (having no other provision) the Indian was eaten up, and Janvier determined to have human flesh if no other could be obtained. To this end he sought an opportunity to quarrel with St. Ange—Dufresne not daring to interfere in the dispute. Janvier willing, however, to appear as plausible in the eyes of Dufresne as possible, widened the breach very artfully, till pretending he was no longer able to contain his anger, asked Dufresne if he did not think St. Ange deserved the Indian's fate, for daring to say he would reveal the circumstance he had so solemnly sworn to conceal. Dufresne dreading the consequences of differing with him in sentiment, said he thought St. Ange was to blame; upon which reply, Janvier immediately struck him with an axe, and killed him: he then cut him up, and boiled a part, of which he obliged Dufresne to partake, he not daring to shew any reluctance. Fortunately for Dufresne the weather became more moderate, and having caught plenty of fish, they proposed to return to their master. Janvier, intoxicated with ideas of his superiority, obliged Dufresne to drag him in an Indian slay to Mr. Fulton's house—a cruel imposition upon him, and a dreadful service to a weak emaciated man! but knowing he was unable to resist, he made a virtue of necessity, and obeyed the tyrant with seeming cheerfulness. On the journey he was frequently reminded of his oath, and the fatal consequences that would attend him if he should ever divulge the secret, which Janvier assured him would produce instant death.

Mr. Fulton was much rejoiced at their return, being in want of his men, as the Indians were daily coming in with their winter hunt. Soon after their arrival he made enquiry after St. Ange—but no answer was given. He then addressed Janvier directly upon the subject, who said he was gone on the hunt with a chief of the name of *Onnemay*, or the Sturgeon, whom Mr. Fulton knew, and that he would soon return. One of the Canadians contradicted him by saying that could not be true, as *Onnemay* left Mr. Fulton's house the day before their return. Janvier then said he might be mistaken in the chief's name, as he was not well acquainted with the Indian language, and Dufresne, for fear of a discovery at that time, changed the conversation in hopes of pleasing Janvier.

Several days elapsed, and St. Ange not returning, Janvier was again questioned, who told them as before, and appealed to Dufresne for the truth of his assertions, which he was obliged to confirm.

Mr. Fulton not being perfectly satisfied, examined them apart; from Janvier he could not get any information, but Dufresne hesitated, and at last said he had sworn not to reveal—but that St. Ange would never return.—Mr. Fulton endeavoured to convince him that the breach of an oath, so imposed, was no crime; and in the end he convinced the Canadian that it was so far from being obligatory in the sight of God, that it would be a sin of the most heinous nature in him to conceal the truth; artfully adding, as an additional argument to induce him to reveal the transaction, that if he had no doubt he was himself perfectly innocent, he could not have any honest motive for secrecy, and that he had no occasion to dread the resentment of Janvier, as he would engage to protect him from all hazard by the discovery. Thus persuaded and encouraged, Dufresne disclosed the whole affair, but requested Mr. Fulton's secrecy, which he promised until the conversation should be renewed, when it was agreed that he should relate every particular in Janvier's presence. Janvier was repeatedly urged by the rest of the men to give them some information respecting the absence of St. Ange, but he remained obstinately silent: some of them went so far as to accuse him in pretty plain terms of knowing too much about him, but he treated their insinuations with indifference.

Mr. Fulton having disposed of all his goods, prepared to leave his wintering ground, and every thing being properly arranged they departed. The first night after their departure Mr. Fulton loaded a brace of pistols, and having previously acquainted his men with the discovery Dufresne had made, and the punishment he intended for the villain, came out of his tent and stood by the fire round which the Canadians were seated. The conversation about St. Ange being purposely renewed, Mr. Fulton remarked it was cruel to leave him in the woods with the Indians, and blamed Janvier particularly, as he was the foreman of the party, and therefore the more responsible. Janvier nettled at the repetition of the subject, (for guilt is soon angry) replied that St. Ange was able to take care of himself, and that he had not any controul over him. Dufresne was then censured; upon which, agreeably to the plan settled with Mr. Fulton, he divulged the whole transaction, and gave a full account of every particular of Janvier's conduct. Janvier attempted to take instant revenge for the aspersion, as he called it, and denied the charge with the most hardened effrontery and solemn asseverations. Mr. Fulton then thought it a proper time

to interfere; and to cover him if possible with confusion, asked him
" which was the best part of a man?" Janvier replied, with ready in-
solence, that those who had eaten human flesh could easily tell: but being repeatedly urged, and at length thrown off his guard, he replied
in great wrath, the feet. The party encouraged by this confession,
pressed the charge, till at last he confessed the facts he was accused of,
and declared that in a similar situation he would kill his brother.

Mr. Fulton could no longer suppress his resentment, and going up
to Janvier, told him he was an abandoned villain, first for killing a
harmless Indian who had generously relieved his wants, and afterwards
eating him like a cannibal; that not content with these atrocious acts,
he had encreased his guilt by another deliberate murder on a defenceless
man, his companion, his fellow-labourer, and friend; that he was a disgrace to human nature, and ought not to be suffered to live a moment
longer; and without allowing him time to reply, shot him through the
head. The men were ordered to bury him, and in the morning Mr.
Fulton continued his journey to *Michillimakinac*, where on his arrival
he surrendered himself to the commanding officer, who on a close examination of the men, honourably acquitted him; but recommended him
not to venture again into those parts, where the Indian was killed,
lest the Savages should hear of the transaction, and resent the death of
one of their tribe, whereby the innocent might suffer for the acts of
the guilty.

In the month of February I had a visit from a trader, dressed in a
smoked leather shirt; who was accompanied by three Indians, and had been
absent five days from Fort Albany. He said he was induced to come

from a motive of curiosity to see me, not having heard of any person wintering so far inland before, except the servants belonging to the Hudson's Bay Company. At that time I had very little provisions, and eight men to maintain, besides Mr. Joseph La Forme's Canadians; our chief food was *tripe de roche*; on his arrival the kettle was on the fire with the leaves: he asked what food I had; I ordered some to be taken out of the pot, and put into a bark dish, which he tasted, but could not swallow. I informed him that it had been a principal part of our diet for many days, and in the best of times we had nothing but wild animal food, and seldom any flour, as the quantity of Indian corn we were able to bring along with us from Pays Plat was not sufficient to last the winter. When I had given him a description of my mode of living, which he confessed was very different from the comforts he enjoyed, I took him into my store, and shewed him the packs of beaver I had collected: this increased his surprise, as he could not conceive how it was possible to transport a sufficient quantity of goods to barter for the value I seemed to be in possession of. He asked me to return with him, and promised to supply me with provisions; but I told him I was engaged in an employ, and had supported the same disagreeable situation the preceding winter at Lac la Mort; and as I could not expect to pass my life among the Indians with so much ease as in England, my duty obliged me to remain till the season was over, when I should return and endeavour to make myself some amends for the hardships I had endured, by giving a good account of the merchandise intrusted to my care, and receiving a reward for my labours. In the morning he took his leave, wishing me the speedy arrival of some Indians who might be able to relieve me from such pressing necessity by supplying me with plenty of more nourishing and palatable food.

This civility from one of the Hudson's Bay Company's servants leads me to make some few observations in vindication of that respectable body, whose character has been so severely, and I think so unjustly, censured.

Mr. Joseph Robson, one of the company's servants, who resided in their factory six years as surveyor and supervisor of the buildings, in a work published by him some years since, animadverts in very strong terms on the mode in which the governors of forts exert what he calls their uncontroulable authority, and asserts that their extreme tyranny is a perpetual source of personal disgust. He also says, that " the over-" plus trade is big with iniquity, and no less inconsistent with the com-" pany's true interest, than it is injurious to the natives, who by means " of it are become more and more alienated, and are either discouraged " from hunting at all, or induced to carry all their furs to the French." It may be necessary here to observe, that the overplus trade arises from the peltry which the company's servants obtain in barter with the natives beyond the ratio stipulated by the company, and which belongs to themselves.

This is a heavy charge, and, if true, a very proper cause of complaint; but it should seem there is not sufficient ground for the accusation, for Mr. Robson afterwards says that this overplus trade is of little advantage to them, for " that part of it, they always add to the company's " stock, for the sake of enhancing the merit of their services, and apply " the remainder to their own use, which is often expended in bribes to " skreen their faults, and continue them in their command." What a strange degree of folly, as well as of guilt! that the governors are so weak and so wicked as to commit enormities only to make a temporary advantage, and are obliged to distribute the wages of iniquity in order to skreen themselves from its consequences among the company, and their confederates in vice; whereas by a contrary conduct they would be equally rich, more respected, and also feel an inward satisfaction of mind from the consciousness of having discharged their trust with integrity; ideas too absurd to be admitted. With regard to the company, it cannot be supposed they are ignorant of this " overplus trade," or the means by which their servants obtain the advantages arising from it; if they are not, and no impartial person will suppose they are, they not only allow but approve of the conduct of their governors, from a conviction of its being beneficial to the interests of the company; a proper reward for the labours of their servants, or from some other motive, which because it is adopted by men so respectable, and so much above reproach, must be allowed to be wise and prudent.

In the next place, I believe it will be very difficult to prove that the conduct of the governors has " alienated the natives from the company's "interest, and discouraged them from hunting." The former is at present by no means clear, as I am credibly informed the New Northwest Company, whose trade extends to the boundaries of the settlements of the Hudson's Bay Company, find very little encouragement from the Indians; if therefore the natives were disgusted, they would embrace the first opportunity of shewing their dislike, by carrying their peltry to the new traders; nothing can be more natural than to expect that this would be the consequence; but as they have not done so, the inference is fair that they are not disgusted.

Another observation is, " that the cruel and oppressive behaviour of " the governors and captains towards the inferior servants, not only de- " ters useful people from engaging in the company's service (a circum- " stance they should attend to for their own interest), but furnishes one " pretext for the bad character that is given of the company."

Though in the particular department in which I have been many years engaged as an Indian interpreter and trader, I have had few opportunities of a personal and intimate acquaintance with many of the company's servants (having been in a commerce in direct opposition to their interest), yet I can speak with confidence in regard to some of them whom I have conversed with; that in every point of view I believe them to be useful servants, and well skilled in the language of the natives.—So far in answer to the assertion " that useful people are deter- " red from entering into the service." And by way of refuting the charge of " cruelty and oppression," I need only add, what none I think will deny, that they have been so well satisfied with the conduct of their superiors, that many of them have continued in the service more than twenty years.

I believe, upon the whole, it will appear that the conduct of the governors at home and abroad, is perfectly consistent with the true interests of the company, and that any other mode of behaviour would tend to anarchy and confusion; and I must declare for my own part that I never heard of that personal disgust which Mr. Robson so much complains of, but have rather found an anxious solicitude to be employed in their service.

Mr. Carver, in his history of North America, observes, " that on
" the waters which fall into Lake Winnepeek, the neighbouring nations
" take a great many furs, some of them they carry to the Hudson's
" Bay Company's factories, situated at the entrance of the Bourbon
" River, but this they do with reluctance on several accounts ; for
" some of the *Assinipoils* and *Killistinoe* Indians, who usually traded
" with the company's servants, told him that if they could be sure of a
" constant supply of goods from *Michillimakinac*, they would not
" trade any where else; that they shewed him some cloth, and other
" articles purchased at Hudson's Bay, with which they were much
" dissatisfied, thinking they had been greatly imposed on in the
" barter."

To this Mr. Carver adds, " that allowing their accounts true, he
" could not help joining in their opinion;" but afterwards he admits
" that this dissatisfaction might probably proceed, in a great measure,
" from the intrigues of the Canadian traders; and that the method they
" took to withdraw the Indians from their attachment to the Hudson's
" Bay Company, and to engage their good opinion in behalf of their new
" employers, was by depreciating, on all occasions, the company's goods,
" and magnifying the advantages that would arise to them from traffick-
" ing entirely with the Canadian traders: in this they too well succeed-
" ed; and from this, doubtless, did the dissatisfaction which the *Assini-*
" *poils* and *Killistinoes* proceed." But, says he, further, " another
" reason augmented it, the length of the journey to the Hudson's Bay
" Factories, which they informed him took up three months during the
" summer heats to go and return, and from the smallness of their ca-
" noes they could not carry more than one-third of the beaver they

" killed, so that it is not to be wondered at that the Indians should
" wish to have traders come to reside among them." As Mr. Carver
did not travel in the interior parts as a trader, he could not have any
interested commercial motives; on that account he is certainly entitled to credit as an impartial observer : the public will judge of his remarks, and how far they tend to censure, or approve, the conduct of
the Hudson's Bay Company.

I am induced to indulge this digression in consequence of a new
publication on the present state of Hudson's Bay by Mr. Umfreville.

It has unfortunately happened that the company's enemies have been
frequently of their own household, persons in whom they placed confidence
and entrusted the mysteries of their commerce. Differences will naturally arise, and doubtless have arisen between the governors and their
servants, in which case no man is, or ought to be, obliged to stay in a
service that is disagreeable to him; but then it is certainly sufficient to
leave the employ, and highly improper to endeavour to prejudice the
interest he once thought and felt it is duty to promote; and I am of
opinion that not a single transaction, or circumstance, should be revealed that has not an immediate reference to the cause of the disagree-
ment, or is necessary to support or vindicate a reputation. The present governors are men of great probity, and probably may not conde-
scend to take notice of these heavy charges against them; but as the
most exalted virtue may be injured by groundless assertions, I trust
the public will not be displeased with any endeavours, however feeble,
to vindicate the character of so respectable a body. As I do not intend
to enter on the subject more fully, I shall only entreat the reader, if

he wishes further satisfaction on this head, to peruse the publication of Mr. Robson, who was one of the company's servants, and who, Mr. Umfreville acknowledges to be a true and impartial writer. From his account the reader will judge of the propriety of Mr Umfreville's censures on the conduct of the governors of the Hudson's Bay Company. A more copious examination of Mr. Umfreville's publication would exceed the limits I have prescribed to myself; and I cannot but think that those who peruse it will readily perceive how much injustice he has done to the governors and the company.

Arrival of more Indians.—Rum gets short; adopt the usual Mode to encrease the Stock, which enables us to conclude our Traffic for the Season.—Take leave of the Indians, and proceed on our Journey homewards.—Account of an Indian Courtship.—Servile State of the Women after Marriage.—Observations on the Confidence which the Indians put in the Master of Life,—&c.—Arrive safe at Pays Plat.

Soon after the departure of the trader, a large band, consisting of about 100, came in; my stock of rum was very small, which was a misfortune, as rum is too important in treaties with the Indians to be easily dispensed with. On their arrival they wished to drink, but I continued to barter for all their furs before I gave them any rum: having finished the business, they grew clamorous, when I gave them as much rum as I could spare, upon receipt of which they embarked in tolerable good humour.

In the month of April the last band came in, and I was extremely perplexed how to act, having a very small portion of rum, and no prospect of encreasing my stock; I was therefore obliged to dilute it so as to make it about one-fifth part weaker than usual, which made twenty gallons of very passable Indian rum. Having supplied them with wearing apparel, &c. and received their peltry, I gave them a taste of the *scuttaywabo*, and just before my embarkation made the following speech:

"*Haguarmissey cockinnor an Nisbinnorbay kee wabindan cawwick-
"car nin serpargussey nee zargetoone, keennerwind kaygo kee cusbken-
"dum webatch neeunerwind tercusbenan nepewar annacotchigon nin ojey
"petoone. Wa baguarmissey cockinnor meenwendesay baxam Ebeck-
"check megoyyach debwoye neegee kaygo arwayyor matchee oathly, kee
"cannawendan cockinnor, mokoman, baskeyzegan goyer becka, kee min-
"niquy kaygo arwayyor annascartissey woke, mornooch kee permartis-
"syan cockinnor an Nisbinnorbay nogome debwoye negee nepewar ar-
"tawway winnin ojey zargetoone an Nisbinnorbay, keshpin suggermarch
"wennewar metach nin ojey debarchemon hitchee ojemaw awassa woity
"kitchee wakaygan Michbillimakinac metach kaygoshish ween ojey bocket-
"tywaun keennerwind.*

" Now, my friends, take courage, I have always shewn you a
" good heart, and you all know I am full of pity for you, your
" wives, and children; therefore do not be uneasy, or think the
" time long I shall be absent from you. I hope the Master of
" Life will give me courage and strength to return to you, and
" bring you goods. Now, as you know I have no sugar on my
" lips, nor any spear at my tongue, and that my ears are not stopt, nor
" my heart bound up, I hope you will deliver up your knives, guns,
" and tomahawks, and have no bad heart before you begin to drink,
" so that on my return I may find you all well. I shall speak with

"courage to the great English chief, at *Michillimakinac*, and he will "open his heart to you."

Having finished my speech, the weapons were collected and delivered to me. I then gave them a considerable quantity of rum, after which I returned their knives, &c. to convince them of the good opinion I entertained of them, and that I had no doubt but they would attend to the advice I had given them. I then got into my canoe, and waving my hand, was saluted by a discharge of 200 guns, which I returned by one volley, and pursued my journey in good spirits, heartily pleased at leaving my winter quarters.

We continued our voyage without meeting with any occurrence worth relating till we arrived at the Skunk's River, where I had unfortunately shot off a chief's ear, as I have before related. Here I met with the new-married couple, and some of the same band to whom I was so much obliged in the preceding December for singing the love-songs; and being desirous of obtaining a perfect knowledge of their manners and customs, I made many inquiries, and among other knowledge gained information of the Chippeway form of courtship, which I presume will be acceptable to those who have as much curiosity as myself.

INDIAN COURTSHIP.

When an Indian wishes to take a wife, and sees one to his mind, he applies to the father of the girl, and asks his consent in the following words:

"*Nocey, cunner kee darmissey kee darniss nee zargayyar hakaygo O waterwarwardoossin cawween peccan weetley gammat ottertassey memarjis mee mor.*"

"Father, I love your daughter, will you give her to me, that the small roots of her heart may entangle with mine, so that the strongest wind that blows shall never separate them."

If the father approves, an interview is appointed, for which the lover prepares by a perspiration; he then comes into her presence, sits down on the ground, and smokes his pipe: during the time of smoking, he keeps throwing small pieces of wood, of about an inch in length at her one by one to the number of one hundred. As many as she can catch in a bark bowl, so many presents her lover must make to her father, which he considers as payment for his daughter. The young warrior then gives a feast, to which he invites all the family—when the feast is done, they dance and sing their war songs.—The merriment being over, and mutual presents exchanged between the lover and her relations, the father covers them with a beaver robe, and gives them likewise a new gun and a birch canoe, with which the ceremony ends.

When the French became masters of Canada, the ceremony of marriage between the Savages was very fantastical.

When a lover wished his mistress to be informed of his affection, he procured an interview with her, which was always at night, and in the presence of some of her friends; this was conducted in the following manner:

He entered the *wigwam*, the door of which was commonly a skin, and went up to the hearth on which some hot coals were burning; he then lighted a stick of wood, and approaching his mistress, pulled her *three* times by the nose, to awaken her; this was done with decency, and being the custom, the squaw did not feel alarmed at the liberty. This ceremony, ridiculous as it may appear, was continued occasionally for *two* months, both parties behaving during the time in all other respects, with the greatest circumspection.

The moment she becomes a wife, she loses her liberty, and is an obsequious slave to her husband, who never loses sight of his prerogative. Wherever he goes she must follow, and durst not venture to incense him by a refusal, knowing that if she neglects him, extreme punishment, if not death, ensues. The chief liberty he allows her is to dance and sing in his company, and is seldom known to take any more notice of her than of the most indifferent person: while she is obliged to perform the drudgery of life, which custom or insensibility enables her to do with the utmost cheerfulness.

A circumstance of this kind I recollect reading which happened at Beaver Creek, about twenty-five miles from Fort Pitt. An Indian woman observing some white men to carry fire-wood on their shoulders, took up her hatchet, and brought them in a short time a great burden on her back; and throwing it down by the fire, said, she not only pitied

T

them, but thought it was a great scandal to see men doing that which was properly the work of women.

The men consider women as of no other use but to produce them children, and to perform the drudgeries of life ; as to the offspring, he prefers the sons to the daughter, because he expects they will all prove warriors. The daughters they do not value for the same reason that they subjugate their wives, deeming them worthy only to wait on warriors and do those things which would disgrace the male sex.

We pursued our journey to Lac le Nid au Corbeau, where we killed some wild geese and ducks, which at this season of the year have a fishy taste. Here we rested two days to enable us to pursue the remainder of our voyage with greater vigour. The third morning, at day-break, we embarked, and arrived at La grande Côte de la Roche, where we were fortunate enough to kill two bears, which eat remarkably fine, and having some leisure time to spare in the cookery, we enjoyed them with as high a relish as in better situations we had done more luxuriant meals.

We proceeded to Cranberry Lake, where we caught some fish, and picked as many cranberries as we could conveniently carry; from thence we continued our route to Portage la Rame, where we were again wind-bound for some days; but during our stay we had not a single visitor to disturb us. At length the wind proving favourable, we proceeded to Rivière la Pique; on my arrival I was immediately struck with the remembrance of the escape I had from Payshik Ogashey last year; but my mind was almost as instantly relieved by the recollection of his being killed, and no longer a terror to traders.

This was one among many instances in which I found that when the heart is oppressed with unpleasant recollections, or forebodings, the Author of our Being conveys relief to the mind very unexpectedly. This sudden transition we are too apt to impute to our own wisdom, and to attribute the escape from dangers we have experienced, or the hopes of deliverance which we form, entirely to our own sagacity and foresight. The Indians, on the contrary, think more properly; they say it is the Master of Life from whom we derive that presence of mind which has extricated or procured us relief. To the Master of Life the Indian addresses himself even for his daily support.—To him he imputes his victories and his success; and when subdued, and fastened to the stake, he thanks him for giving him courage to open his veins.—It is this confidence which enables him to bear the severest tortures with composure, and in the height of anguish, to defy the utmost malice of his enemies.

Notwithstanding the Chippeways, as well as the greater part of the Indian nations, of North America, think so justly, it is to be lamented that it is not universally so. The *Mattaugwessawauks*, it is said, do not worship a Supreme Being, and that when success attends them in war, they attribute the merit of the victory to their own valour and skill. But notwithstanding their disbelief of a Master of Life, in some respects, they are not less superstitious than other Savages, for they think that certain places are haunted by evil spirits, whose power they dread, and impressed with these ideas cautiously avoid them. Another proof of their superstition is, if one of their people is killed by accident, they preserve a hand or a foot, which they salt, and dry, and keep as a charm to avert calamities; by which it appears, that although they do not acknowledge a dependance on a good spirit, they entertain fears and apprehensions of a bad one; which induces one to hope that such a deviation from the common belief of mankind may never be confirmed, as it would stamp human nature with an odium too horrid to think of. But to conclude this digression—we continued our voyage to Pays Plat, where we stayed some days in the society of traders, who had also wintered in the islands, and others who arrived with goods to supply those who were engaged to return; but as my time was expired, I returned to *Micbillimakinac*. After waiting on the commanding officer, and giving an account of my stewardship to my employers, I retired to Chippeway Point, a spot of ground out of the Fort, where I lived with an Indian family, who occasionally made me *mackissins*,. and other parts of Indian dress.

THIRD EXPEDITION.

Remain some Time at Chippeway Point.—Account of a whimsical Circumstance, whereby I had nearly incurred the Displeasure of the Commanding Officer.—Narrative of the fortunate Escape of a Mr. Ramsay, a Trader.—Undertake to escort a Quantity of Merchandise from the Mississippi to Michillimakinac, which I perform with Success.—Return to Montreal; from thence to Quebec, where I engage with a new Employer.

During the time I remained at Chippeway Point, I had frequent offers from the officers to sleep at their quarters within the fort; but being accustomed to lie in the woods, I generally preferred that situation. A circumstance happened soon after my arrival, which I shall relate.

In consequence of Indian treachery in the year 1764, (when the Savages, commanded by *Pontiac* the chief, under the pretence of a game at ball, formed a plan to destroy the inhabitants, and take possession of the fort, and in which they unfortunately succeeded, to the extreme mortification of the English), there was a standing order that no Indian should be permitted to enter the fort with fire-arms; nor any squaw, or Indian woman, allowed to sleep within the walls of the garrison on any pretence whatever; and for the better security of the inhabitants, when a council is held with the chiefs, double sentries are always placed.

Having a strong desire to introduce a great chief's daughter and her sister, (notwithstanding the governor's orders) I communicated my intentions to an officer, and desired his assistance to complete the plan. He very politely told me that he could not appear to countenance my scheme, but would give me every possible assistance consistent with his station. I assured him that they were a great chief's daughters, and that I would be answerable for their conduct.

With his consent I applied to two soldiers, and asked them if they could spare time to roll a large hogshead of bottled porter from Chippeway Point to the Fort; they told me whenever it suited me they would be ready to assist. Having purchased the hogshead, and got it rolled down the hill whilst the officers were at dinner, I told the squaws of my plan, and having knocked out the head and bung, and bored several holes to admit as much air as possible, desired them to get in, which with some difficulty I persuaded them to do. I then replaced the head, and ran immediately to the soldiers to acquaint them that the porter was ready, and desired their assistance without delay, as I was afraid some of the bottles were broken, and it would be proper to examine them as soon as possible.

The soldiers immediately returned with me, and applying their shoulders to the cask, rolled it up the hill with great labour and fatigue, continually observing that it was very heavy. Just as they arrived at the gate, the commanding officer and the commissary were coming through, and seeing the hogshead, asked the soldiers what they had got there? they replied it was bottled porter for a trader, who had desired them to roll it from the Point. As a vessel had just then arrived from the Détroit, the commanding officer was so satisfied with the account the soldiers gave, that he observed it was very fortunate, for they now should have plenty of good beer to drink. The soldiers had scarcely rolled another turn, when unluckily one of them kicked his foot against a stone, who with the extreme pain he suffered, fell down. The other, not being able to sustain the whole weight, let go his hold, and the hogshead rolled down the hill with great velocity. Just as it came to the bottom the head fell out, and the squaws exhibited the deception. Unfortunately the commanding officer was near at hand when the accident happened, and though it was a manifest breach of his orders, he could not help smiling at the conceit; and looking at the imprisoned females, said to them, " pretty bottled porter indeed!" The squaws were so confused that they ran with the utmost precipitation into the woods, and did not make their appearance for several days.

On the commanding officer's return to the fort, enquiry was made for me, and I was under the necessity of obeying his summons, although I confess my situation was very unpleasant. As soon as I came into his presence, assuming a look of displeasure, he asked me how I could dare to disobey the orders of the garrison, which I knew were issued to prevent the most serious consequences ; that I was more culpable than another person, knowing the nature and disposition of the Indian women, and the impropriety and danger of confiding in them, adding that for the sake of example, and to prevent others from acting so imprudently, he believed he should send me down to Montreal in irons.

Alarmed at my situation, I made the best apology in my power, and assured him I was extremely sorry for my conduct, but hoped he would pardon it. This acknowledgment of the offence induced him to forgive me, and as he said he considered it a frolic of youth, he would pass it over, but cautioned me against playing such tricks again. I felt myself extremely obliged by his lenity, and promised to conduct myself with more propriety in future, which promise I faithfully kept: for though the experiment to admit the squaws would not have been attended with any bad consequences, I did not chuse again to risk the commanding officer's displeasure.

On the 11th of August, the traders arrived from the *Mississippi*, and brought an account of an extraordinary escape which a Mr. Ramsay and his brother had from a tribe of the nation of the Poes, in their way to St. Joseph.

The Poes are a very wild savage people, have an aversion to Englishmen, and generally give them as much trouble as possible in passing or repassing the Fort of St. Joseph's, where some French traders are settled by their permission.

It seems the Canadians were invited by the Savages to land, and Mr. Ramsay supposing they had some furs to dispose of, ordered his men to go on shore; when standing up in his canoe just before his debarkation, three of the warriors waded through the water neck-high, dragged him out of his canoe, and carried him on shore. Mr. Ramsay's men immediately landed, and were preparing to follow their master, but observing eleven Indians near at hand, and perceiving the bad intention of the chiefs, got again into their canoes, leaving the one in which Mr. Ramsay and his son were, on the beach, and paddled to an adjacent island, waiting the event of a circumstance which threatened death to their masters.

Mr. Ramsay being tied to the stump of a tree, and his son narrowly watched, the Indians rummaged the canoe, and brought up as much rum as they thought they could drink; they then began to sing their war songs; and making a large fire near the stump to which Mr. Ramsay was tied, they sat down on the ground, and began to insult him, telling him he was an old woman, and obliged his brother to join in the derision.

The usual mode of execution among the Savages, is as follows:

When a warrior is taken, he is brought into a hut, and tied with small cords made of the bark of trees, about the size of a cod-line: he is then fastened to a stump, and a small rattle put into his hand, called *chessaquoy*, which he shakes while he sings the dead war song:

"*Wabindan paysbih shemagonish hitchee mannitoo; nee wee waybe-*
"*nan nee yoe Matchee Mannitoo.*

"Master of Life, view me well as a warrior; I have thrown away my "body against the bad spirit."

When the song is finished, the prisoner is untied, and made to run the gauntlet through two ranks of women, who are provided with small sticks to beat him. After this punishment a dog-feast is prepared with bear's grease and huckleberries, of which he is obliged to eat. He is then brought again to the stake, when wood is placed round him. He now sings his war-song, and the women set fire to the pile, the prisoner singing as it burns. The bones are then collected and fixed to the war-standard, which is a high pole painted with vermillion.

It is said that the nation of the *Followens*, or Wild Oats, kill their wives and children before they go to battle, that in case of a defeat the enemy shall not have any prisoners of their nation.

The Poes, beginning to feel the effects of the rum, examined the cords, which were made of the bark of the willow-tree, and ordered some wood to be put round the stump, to be ready when they should find themselves disposed to burn him. Soon after they untied him, and brought him to the war-kettle to make his death-feast; which consisted of dog, tyger-cat, and bear's grease, mixed with wild oats, of which he was compelled to eat. Mr. Ramsay, knowing the nature of Indians, complied with seeming cheerfulness, and said he was satisfied. He was taken back to the intended place of execution, and tied again to the stump, from which, with great composure, he desired permission to make his speech before he changed his climate, which being granted, he immediately spoke to them to the following effect:

" It is true the Master of Life has sent me here to those Indians whose
" hearts are full of poisoned blood, and as they mean me to change
" my climate, I shall go with courage to a better trading ground, where
" I shall find good Indians. They have always known me to have had
" pity on them, their wives, and children, since I have been a trader,
" and to have opened my heart to them on all occasions; but now the

"bad spirit has joined his heart with theirs, to make me change my cli-
"mate, which I am glad of, for I am better known in the country I
"am going to, and by greater warriors than ever these were. I now
"look on all the chiefs as old women; and as I am the *Peshshekey* (or
"buffalo), I shall drink my last with them, and carry the news to the
"warriors in the other climate."

Having attentively heard his speech, they prepared for his death; which he perceiving, immediately told his brother not to be disheartened, as he had hopes of overcoming their fury, and desired him to ply them with rum, and keep their kettles constantly filled. His brother followed the instructions he gave him, and distributed the rum among them very plentifully. When Mr. Ramsay discovered that they were sufficiently intoxicated to be incapable of doing mischief, he desired his brother to cut his cords; and being released, assisted in pouring rum down their throats till they were quite insensible. Fired with resentment at their intended barbarity, he and his brother cut all their throats, loaded his canoe with the articles they had taken out, and paddled from shore as fast as they could. The men hailed him at some distance, and were rejoiced to see him safe; and after arranging their cargo, pursued their journey into the Indian country, by a different course.

[marginalia: He was worse than the Heathen Ulysses, who only bored out the Savage Polyphemus Eye.— I wish he had not been an Englishman.]

I was informed Mr. Ramsay returned afterwards to *Michillimakinac*, where he was congratulated by the commanding officer on his fortunate escape; but he never thought it prudent to go that route again.

About this time the Indian traders formed a company of militia, which I joined with the rank of adjutant and lieutenant, under Captain

John Macnamara. In the month of June 1780, news was brought from the *Mississippi*, that the Indian traders had deposited their furs at *La Praire des Chiens*, or Dogs' Field, (where there is a town of considerable note, built after the Indian manner) under the care of Mons. Longlad, the king's interpreter; and that the Americans were in great force at the *Illinois*, a town inhabited by different nations, at the back of the Kentuckey State, under the Spanish government, who have a fort on the opposite shore, commanded by an officer and about twelve men, to prevent illicit trade.

The commanding officer at *Michillimakinac* asked me to accompany a party of Indians and Canadians to the *Mississippi*, which I consented to with the utmost cheerfulness. We left the post with thirty-six Southern Indians, of the *Ottigaumies* and *Sioux* nations, and twenty Canadians, in nine large birch canoes, laden with Indian presents. After a march of three days I was taken ill, which I attributed to hard living in the Nipegon Country; considering, however, the urgency of the business, and that there was not any one of the party capable of acting as interpreter, I struggled with my indisposition; apprehending, also, that if I could not pursue the journey, I should be exposed to great inconveniences; and therefore I encreased my endeavours, determined to risk my life at all hazards.

The fourth day we encamped at Lac les Puans, so called, I apprehend, from the Indians who reside on the banks being naturally filthy—here we got plenty of deer and bears, Indian corn, melons and other fruit. The Southern Indians have more villages, and are better civilized than the Northern, the climate being warm, and nature more prolific, which enables them to raise the fruits of the earth without much labour. Their houses are covered with birch bark, and decorated with bows and arrows, and weapons of war. Their beds are bark and matts made of rushes.

We pursued our voyage to *Onisconsin*, a fine River, with a strong current for about sixty leagues, which our canoes ran down in a day and a half; and upon which we saw an immense quantity of ducks, geese, and other fowl. On this river we were obliged to unload our canoes, in order to transport our goods across the portage, about two miles in length. We encamped on the banks, and intended setting off at break of day, but one of the Indians was bitten by a rattlesnake, which Mr. Adair calls the bright inhabitant of the woods, and which had fourteen rattles.

Mr. Beatty relates that as he was preaching to the Indians and others, at a small house near Juniata River, a rattle-snake crept into the room, but was happily discovered and killed; and before the people could well recover themselves, a snake of another kind was discovered among the assembly, which was also killed without any other detriment than disturbing the congregation, which surprised him very much, as it was a matter of astonishment how these reptiles could crawl into the house without being offended by some one, and which always excites them to bite.

The Indians say that when a woman is in labour, holding the tail of a rattle-snake in her hand, and shaking the rattles, assists her delivery. It is always observable that the Indians take out the bag which contains the poison of this venomous reptile, and carry it alive in their medicine box when they go to war.

This unfortunate accident retarded our journey till the unhappy sufferer relieved himself by cutting out the wounded part from the calf of his leg, and applying salt and gunpowder, and binding it up with the leaves of the red willow tree; he was soon able to proceed, bearing the pain with that fortitude for which the Savages are so eminently distinguished.

At the close of the next day we encamped near the river, and it rained very hard: the Indians made some bark huts. One of them walking some distance in the woods, discovered a small loghouse, in which he found a white man, with his arms cut off, lying on his back. We conjectured he had been settled at the spot, and killed by a bad Indian, which must have happened very recently, as he was not putrid. Before our departure we buried him.

The next day we arrived at the Forks of the Mississippi, where were two hundred Indians of the nation of the Renards, or Foxes, on horseback, armed with spears, bows and arrows. They did not seem pleased with our appearance, which *Warbisbar*, the chief of our band, told me. Just before we landed they dismounted, and surveyed us. The Sioux asked me if I was afraid; I told them I had seen a greater number of Savages before, and more wild than any of the Southern Indians. *Warbisbar* gave orders to strike ashore. As soon as we landed, the Renards took our Indians by the hand, and invited them into their camp. In the space of an hour they prepared a feast, which consisted of five

Indian dogs, bear, beaver, deer, mountain cat, and racoon, boiled in bear's grease, and mixed with huckleberries. After the repast, the Indians danced and sung. A council was then held, when the chief of the Renards addressed *Warbishar* to this effect.

" Brothers, we are happy to see you ; we have no bad heart against
" you; although we are not the same nation by language, our hearts
" are the same: we are all Indians, and are happy to hear our great
" Father has pity on us, and sends us wherewithal to cover us, and en-
" able us to hunt."

To which *Warbishar* made answer.—" It is true, my children, our
" great Father has sent me this way to take the skins and furs that
" are in the Dog's Field, under captain Longlad's charge, least the
" Great Knives (meaning the Americans) should plunder them. I am
" come with the white man (meaning me) to give you wherewithal to
" cover you, and ammunition to hunt."

When the speech was finished, we immediately distributed the presents, got our canoes into the water, and left the Renards in the most friendly manner.

After seven days journey we arrived at *La Prairie des Chiens*, where we found the merchants' peltry, in packs, in a loghouse guarded by captain Longlad and some Indians, who were rejoiced to see us. After resting some time, we took out about three hundred packs of the best skins, and filled the canoes. Sixty more which remained, we burnt, to prevent the enemy from taking them, having ourselves no room to stow any more, and proceeded on our journey back to Michillimakinac. About five days after our departure, we were informed that the Americans came to attack us, but to their extreme mortification we were out of their reach. Seventeen days after leaving *La Prairie des Chiens*, we arrived at *Lac les Puans*, where we found a party of Indians encamped. The next day we embarked, and arrived at Michillimakinac, after an absence of eighty days. Soon after my return, I waited on the commanding officer, expecting payment for my services; but was referred for satisfaction to the Indian traders, from whom I never received any compensation.

By this means I was left destitute even of the necessaries of life; but I did not remain long in this uncomfortable situation, for I soon found protection and support among the Indians; but as their assistance would not afford the means to appear in civil society, I was under the necessity of soliciting friendship from the merchants, to enable me to return to Montreal, which I fortunately obtained. I left Michillimakinac in the beginning of September, and arrived at Montreal on the 27th of the same month.

I embraced the first opportunity to call on my old master, expecting to find him in good health, but alas! he had paid the debt of nature, and was succeeded by his nephew, who had been cotemporary clerk with me. He permitted me to lodge at his house for a fortnight, but a few days after my abode with him, my situation being different from what I had experienced during the life of my old master, I asked him to fit me out with an assortment of goods for the Indian trade, and promised to remit him payment in furs. He told me I was welcome to any goods he had in his store that would suit me, but on examining the stock, all the merchandise proper for the Savages was disposed of, and nothing left that would answer any profitable purpose.

I then left his house, returning him thanks for his civility; and having procured pecuniary assistance from a friend, took lodgings in the town, where I stayed some time. I then went to Quebec, where a gentleman accidentally hearing that I was out of employ, and knowing that I could speak the Indian languages, sent for me and engaged me in his service, to go among the Indians at Lake Temiscaming, or any other situation I might think most eligible for commerce.

X

Leave Quebec—Description of the Loretto Indians; some Remarks relative to an Assertion, that the American Indians have no Beards.— Mistake the Mercury Packet of Quebec for an American Privateer. —Proceed on our Journey, and arrive at our Winter Residence.— Description of several Sorts of Snakes.—Meet with great Success, and soon complete our Traffic.—Return to Quebec.

BEING furnished with a proper assortment of merchandise, I left Quebec, and proceeded to Tadousac, which is at the end of the Saguenay River, near the River St. Laurence. About nine miles from Quebec there is a village inhabited by the Loretto Indians, who are properly of the nation of the Hurons. They embraced Christianity, through the means of the Jesuits, and follow the Catholic religion. The women have remarkable good voices, and sing hymns in their own language most charmingly. They cultivate the ground, and bring the produce to market; and in their manners they are the most innocent and harmless of all the Savages in North America. Their houses are decent, and built after the Canadian fashion; they are an exception to the generality of Indians, seldom drinking any spirituous liquors; they are for the most part tall, robust people, and well shaped; have short black hair, which is shaved off the forehead from ear to ear, and wear neither caps nor hats. With regard to their beards, though they are scarcely visible, they have them in common with all the tribes of Savages; but having an aversion to excrescences, they carefully pluck out every hair from the upper jaw and chin with brass wire, which they twist together in the form of pincers; and it is well known that all traders carry out that article of commerce for this express purpose.

Baron de la Hontan seems to have been much mistaken when, in speaking of the Savages, he says that they have no beards. Lord Kaims was also in the same error, when he asserted there is not a single hair on an Indian's body, excepting the eyelashes, eyebrows, and hair of the head, and that there is no appearance of a beard.

This observation Mr. James Adair remarks is utterly void of foundation, as can be attested by all who have had any communication with them; and major Robert Rogers, who certainly knew the Indians as well as any man, says that they *totally destroy* their beards; which proves beyond a doubt that they are not naturally *imbarbes*.

I have been led into these observations from the perusal of Lord Kaims's Sketches of the History of Man, who not only insists that the Indians have no beards, but builds on the hypothesis to prove a local creation.

Tadousac is on the sea side, north of the River St. Laurence, and inhabited by a few Indians called mountaineers, who live chiefly on fish; and one trader, clerk to the gentleman in whose service I was engaged.

There is a French clergyman and a church for the Indians, who are all Catholics. At this village I remained a fortnight, during which time the American privateers were continually cruizing about. One morning there was a great fog, but we could just discern at a small distance a vessel: this alarmed the priest and the Indians. My brother Englishman (the trader who was settled here) joined with me in soliciting the Indians to stand their ground, which the priest strongly opposed, though paid by the British government. This incensed me, and I insisted on taking some of his flock with me to reconnoitre, and endeavour to discover what vessel she was, though I had strong suspicions she was an American privateer. We went towards the shore, but could not discover the number of guns she mounted; we returned to our camp, and all the Indians at my request accompanied me to attack her. We embarked in canoes, dressed alike, and as we approached perceived she lay at anchor, and was a vessel of inconsiderable force, mounting only eight small swivels. I immediately went on one side of her, and directed the Indians to the other, to inclose her as much as we could. Having reached the vessel, I took hold of a rope and went on board; the captain was alarmed, and his fears were increased when he saw himself surrounded with canoes, filled with Savages armed with guns and tomahawks; however, he advanced towards me, and clapping me on the shoulder, asked what I wanted? I was too politic to make any reply at that time. He then asked me, if I would have some biscuit? I replied, *caween*, or no. He shook his head, as much as to say, I wish I could know what you want. The Indians then came on board, and the captain having only seven men, and our number being upwards of forty, well armed, did not know how to act, but, probably willing to please me, ordered his men to get some biscuit and rum. Whilst the sailors were gone, I perceived she was an English vessel, and then asked the captain in English to whom she belonged; he was very agreeably surprised, told me his name was Allcrow, and that he commanded the Mercury Packet of Quebec. This information gave me occasion to rejoice we did not take rough means; and when I communicated the intelligence to the Indians they were highly pleased, and shook hands with the captain.

The captain then accompanied us to shore in our canoes, and we landed at our encampment. We afterwards went to the priest's house, where we dined. Mr. Martin, the priest, and myself were invited on board the next day, when we had an excellent repast, with plenty of wine and other liquors. Unfortunately we drank too freely, and returning in the evening, the priest began to be very angry with me for encouraging the Savages; this reprehension, with his former conduct, incensed me exceedingly, and in the heat of passion I threw him overboard, but by the assistance of the sailors he was saved. On our landing, our contest led us to blows, but we were soon parted. When we were recovered from intoxication, we shook hands, and afterwards remained good friends.

The next day the Indians were seized with an epidemic fever, which deprived them of the use of their limbs, and occasioned a delirium. The disorder attacked me very severely, but by the friendly assistance of Mr. Martin, who had a medicine chest, in about three weeks I recovered.

The winter now advancing very rapidly, and the unavoidable delay at this post, obliged me to proceed on my journey on snow shoes, carrying all my goods on Indian slays, through the woods, and over high mountains. We travelled twenty-one days, on a deep snow, about one hundred leagues through the Saguenay country, which was very fatiguing, till we arrived at a place called Checootimy; about half way up the river on which it stands the salt water ebbs and flows. Only a few Indians reside here, and one Indian trader, with whom I wintered, and hunted, killing a great many animals. Early in the spring I took my leave of him, and being furnished with canoes, pursued my journey to St. John's Lake; from thence to Panebacash River, to Lake Shaboomoochoine, which lies north-east of Lake Arbitibis about the distance of seven days Indian march.

Near the Falls of Panebacash River I landed, and ascended a high mountain, to survey a large cave, about two hundred yards deep, and three yards wide at the mouth. Here I picked up a piece of ore, about three inches square; the exterior crust was black and very thin, and when broke, appeared yellow. I brought it to Quebec, but by some accident lost it, which I lamented exceedingly, as some of my friends to whom I shewed it were of opinion that it was very valuable.

This journey was farther inland, by near eighty leagues, than any trader had ever been, the only settlement in that part of Canada being at St. Peter's Lake, where a French house was formerly established, and where an English trader, who was employed by the merchants in whose service I was engaged, resided.

I arrived at Lake Shaboomoochoine on the 26th of May, 1781, where I intended only to stay a few days; but some Indians arrived who assured me that it would answer my purpose to winter, and promised to supply me with fish, furs, and skins. This induced me to remain here; and I built a house suitable for my business, and kept two Indians with their wives to hunt for me.

On the 29th we set our nets, and in about four hours caught abundance of large trout, pike, maskenonjey, pickerill, and white fish, and as the country abounded with wild fowl, we were never without two courses at table, with roots for garden stuff.

On the 17th of June a band of Indians arrived, who were agreeably surprised to see a trader at a place where no one had settled before, and they were particularly delighted when they heard me speak their own language.

During my residence here I saw a great many snakes; and one day in particular as I was walking in the woods, I discovered one of those reptiles in the grass; the instant I perceived it, I cut a long stick and dropt it gently on the snake's head; it immediately moved, and I could hear the rattles very distinctly. Whilst I was surveying the brightness of its colours, which were inexpressibly beautiful, it was coiling itself round like a rope to dart at me; this warned me of my danger, and I took the taper end of the stick, and let the heavy end fall on its head; the weight of the blow stunned it, and seizing this opportunity, I struck it again, which killed it. I measured it, and judged the length to be at least five feet and an half, and the thickest part about four inches in circumference, with nine rattles on the tail, which agreeable to the general observation, made his age nine years; but I believe this is not an established fact, as it is uncertain at what time the rattle begins to appear.

The flesh of this reptile is delicious, and I have frequently eaten of it with great goût. I have seen the Indians poison it with the juice of tobacco.

Whilst I am on the subject, though not quite connected with it, I shall make some observations on the turkey and black water snake.

The turkey snake is longer than the rattle snake, with stripes on the back, and a spear at the end of its tail like an anchor, and a double row of teeth in each jaw. It takes its name from its voice, which resembles the note of a wild turkey. In the Mississippi it feeds on wild rice, which grows among long grass, bearing its head frequently erect, and makes a noise like a turkey to decoy it; as the bird approaches, the snake darts its tail into it, and makes it an easy prey.

The black water snake is used by the Indians when they go to war; they pull out the teeth, tie the head and tail together, and fasten it round their bodies, which soon kills it. They take it off every night, and put it on every morning.

In travelling from Toniata Creek, on the River St. Laurence to Pimetiscotyan Landing, on Lake Ontario, I saw one of these snakes swimming with a flat fish in its mouth, which I had the good fortune to shoot, and released the prisoner from the jaws of death.

I kept a flag constantly flying at my little fort, which the Indians paid respect to by a salute from their guns. The band who were at this time with me held a council, and made me a present of two very large beaver robes, and several valuable skins, with plenty of provisions, for which I supplied them with tobacco, rum, trinkets, and ammunition. Two days after they left me, and desired me to wait their return, which I promised, provided they would bring me furs and skins to load the canoes, and they should be repaid with Indian goods. As I depended on their punctuality, I remained perfectly satisfied.

I was then left with two white men, and two Indians and their wives. We passed our time in hunting and fishing; and as there were a great many small islands near us, we made frequent trips to shoot wild fowl, which enabled us to keep a good table. On one of the islands we discovered two Indian huts, but from their appearance no person had visited them for a length of time. About half a mile from the place we saw a high pole, daubed over with vermilion paint; on the top were placed three human skulls, and the bones hung round: the Indians supposed it had been erected many years. About an hour before sun set we returned to our wigwam. The next morning, in the absence of the Indians, the Canadians assisted me in mixing the rum, and assorting the goods, to be prepared against the arrival of the Savages, and to fill up the time, which hung heavy on our hands.

On the 24th of June, a band of Indians arrived from Lake Arbitibis, who brought a considerable quantity of excellent furs and skins, with dried meat, which I bartered for. When the bargain was made, I gave them some rum, as usual upon such occasions, which, after their long march, highly delighted them. They drank very plentifully, as I had exceeded the common donation, but their cargo deserved it; and. I always found it my interest to be generous to them upon a barter.

Y

On their departure, taking an Indian for my guide, I made a visit to a brother trader, one hundred and fifty miles from my settlement. I stayed with him about a fortnight, and was on the point of returning, when two Indians came to inform me, by the desire of my Canadians, that a band of Savages waited for me. In about five days we returned, and I bartered for all their furs.

On the 16th of July, about fifty Savages came with their spring hunt, which I also bartered for, though the peltry was very inferior to what is collected in winter; but as I was determined to make as good a season as possible, I was eager to avail myself of every opportunity to increase my stock.

The latter end of the month, the band who had promised to return came in, and fulfilled their promise, bringing a large quantity of furs, which, with the stock I had collected during their absence, was as much as my canoes would hold. They also brought intelligence that the Hudson's Bay Company had been pillaged of their furs by the French.

Early in the month of August I made up my packs, and embarked for Quebec, where I arrived in about six weeks, to the great joy of my employers, who, from my long absence, were very uneasy; however, the cargo fully satisfied them, and convinced them of my industry and integrity in their service. Being persuaded I had undergone great fatigue, they made me a handsome present above my salary, and I quitted their service, and the Indian life, with a resolution to endeavour to procure an employ less hazardous, and where I could partake of the pleasures of society with less fatigue both of body and mind.

I remained some time at Quebec, and intended to pass my winter there, but my money being nearly exhausted, and my mind not reconciled to another Indian voyage, I returned to Montreal, where I found friends to supply my wants till the spring following.

Visit Fort George.—Remarkable Instance of Courage in a Mohawk Indian.—Return to England.—Enter into a new Engagement, and return to Canada, with Merchandise for the Indian Commerce.

IN May I took a trip to Fort George, situated on a lake of the same name, called by the French, *Saint Sacrement,* where I stayed with some of the Mohawks, who were encamped there. In the beginning of the French and Indian war in 1757, there was a remarkable instance of resolution and cool deliberate courage in one of these Savages, occasioned by a sentence being passed upon a soldier to receive five hundred lashes for intoxication.

An Indian known by the name of *Silver Heels,* from his superior agility, as well as his admirable finesse in the art of war, and who had killed more of the enemy than any one of the tribes in alliance with Great Britain, accidentally came into the fort just before the soldier was to receive his punishment, and expressed his displeasure that a man should be so shamefully disgraced. He went up to the commanding officer, and asked him what crime the soldier had committed: the officer not chusing to be questioned, ordered one of his men to send Silver Heels away, and to inform him that the company of Indians was not agreeable on such occasions; *Wa! wa!* or, Oh! oh! replied the Savage, but what is the warrior tied up for? For getting drunk, answered the soldier:—Is that all? said Silver Heels, then provide another set of halberts, and tie up your chief, for he gets drunk twice a day. Having said so, he instantly left the fort, telling the soldier he should quickly return, to endeavour to prevent the punishment being inflicted. Soon after the delinquent was tied up, and the drummers in waiting to obey orders, Silver Heels returned; and going up to the officer, with a tomahawk and scalping knife, said to him, Father, are you a warrior, or do you only think yourself so? If you are brave, you will not suffer your men to strike this soldier whilst I am in this fort. Let me advise you not to spill the good English blood which to-morrow may be wanted to oppose an enemy.—The officer, turning upon his heel, answered with an indignant look, that the soldier had transgressed, and must be flogged.—Well! replied Silver Heels, then flog him, and we shall soon see whether you are as brave a warrior as an Indian.

About two days after the officer was riding some distance from the fort, and Silver Heels was lying flat on his stomach, according to his usual custom when he watched to surprize an enemy. The officer passed without perceiving him, when he instantly sprung up, and laying hold of the horse's bridle, told the officer to dismount and fight him. The officer judging it improper to risk his life against a Savage, refused to dismount, and endeavoured to spur his horse. Silver Heels perceiving his intention, tomahawked the horse, who fell down suddenly, and the officer rolled on the ground without being hurt. Now, says Silver Heels, we are on equal terms, and, as you have a brace of pistols and a sword, you cannot have any objection to fight me. The officer still refusing, Silver Heels told him, that he thought himself a warrior when he ordered one of his white slaves to be flogged for a breach of martial law, but that he had now forgot the character he then assumed, or he certainly would have fought him: and looking very sternly, added, that he had a great mind to make him change his climate; but as that mode of proceeding would not answer his purpose, and sufficiently expose him among his brother warriors, he might walk home as soon as he pleased; and that to-morrrow morning he would come to the fort with the horse's scalp, and relate the circumstance. The officer was rejoiced to escape so well, though he was obliged to walk a distance of three miles.

The next morning Silver Heels arrived, and asked to see the officer, but was denied admission into his presence. Some of his brother officers came out, and enquired his business; he related to them the circumstance between the officer and himself, and exhibited the trophy; adding, that to-morrow he intended going to war, and should make a point of taking an old woman prisoner, whom he should send to take the command of the fort, as the great chief was only fit to fight with his dog, or cat, when he was eating, lest they should have more than him. Then asking for some rum (which was given him), he left the fort to fulfil his promise, but was soon after killed in an engagement, fighting manfully at the head of a party of Mohawks, near the Bloody Pond, joining to Lord Loudon's road, in the way to Albany.

Just before the frost set in, I returned to Montreal, and visited my old Cahnuaga friends, where I amused myself in the Indian way, as I always preferred their society to the Canadians; notwithstanding, I occasionally mixed in more civilized amusements, and as I danced tolerably well, my company was generally sought after.

The Canadians are particularly fond of dancing, from the *seigneur* to the *habitant*; and though the meaner sort of people do not excel in it, there is a peculiar ease, and careless indifference, which, though it appears too rustic, is far from being disagreeable. The beverage on these occasions is sour Spanish red wine, called black strap; and this, homely as it would be thought in more refined assemblies, is there considered as a very handsome manner of treating their friends.

The winter being passed, I determined to go to Quebec, and endeavour to get a passage to England, not having any prospect of a permanent settlement in Canada. On my arrival I put up at a tavern, and lived as moderately as possible, from necessity more than inclination; for every one knows that Indian traders, like sailors, are seldom sufficiently prudent to save much money. Fortunately for me, I met with an old school-fellow at Quebec, a captain of a ship, whom I had not seen for sixteen years. To him I communicated my distressed situation, and by him was generously relieved. In addition to this act of kindness, he promised me a free passage to England on board his vessel, which offer I accepted with pleasure and gratitude.

Having fixed the time of his departure, I took the post, and went to Montreal to settle my affairs: I then returned to Quebec, from whence we sailed the 11th day of October, 1783, and put into Newfoundland. When we came in sight of harbour, several of us requested permission to take the long boat, and row on shore, which was granted; but it being a dead calm, we made very little way. We had not left the ship more than a league, when a south-west wind sprang up, and retarded us considerably. In the evening the wind abated, and with hard rowing we reached the shore about midnight, both fatigued and hungry. Early in the morning the ship came into harbour, and had suffered some damage by beating about in the night, which induced the captain to dispose of the cargo. On the 9th of November we left Newfoundland, on board another vessel: our passage was favourable, without any remarkable occurrence, and we arrived in London the 30th of the same month.

My native city, upon my arrival, appeared like a new world to me, having been absent from England fifteen years; and it was with difficulty I found any of my old friends, the greatest part of them in such a length of time being dead.

In February, 1784, I entered into an engagement with a relation to return to Canada; and being furnished with a cargo, left London on the 15th of April following. On the 20th we got under weigh, and put into Portsmouth, to take in wines. After a bad and tedious passage of eleven weeks, we arrived safe at Quebec, from whence my goods were sent to Montreal in small craft. Unfortunately the season was too far advanced to suffer me to attempt going to Michillimakinac, and wintering in the inlands, as I had no prospect of providing suitable canoes; nor were my goods properly assorted, and there was not time sufficient to arrange them, so as to make the intended voyage. This induced me to consult a friend upon the occasion, who advised me to dispose of my goods at public vendue, which I did, at very great loss, so that I could only remit my friend in London a very small sum in part of payment. In this adventure nothing succeeded to my wishes, for by my credulity, and being willing to retrieve, if possible, the loss I had sustained, I soon increased my difficulties, so that in a few months after my arrival, all my schemes failing, I was left totally destitute.

In February, 1785, I quitted Montreal, and walked from La Prairie to St. John's, where I accidentally found a friend who supplied me with money to go to New York. I proceeded to Stony Point, where I stayed two days with some loyalist officers, some of whom accompanied me to Crown Point, where we also stayed three days. We then parted company, and I hired a slay, which carried me safely to New York, where I took a lodging, and lived as moderately as I could.

During my residence there, I met a Loretto Savage, called Indian John, who had been in the American service all the war, and who waited to receive a reward for his fidelity, as the Congress were then sitting. He told me he had been at war for them nine years, had killed a great many of their enemies, and had only received a gun, two blankets, three pieces of Indian gartering, and one hundred dollars in paper money, which he could not make use of; and as I understood his language, he desired me to render him service by interpreting for him to the governor. I desired him to call at my lodgings, and in the mean time I wrote down the circumstances he had related to me, that I might be prepared, in case I was sent for at a short notice.

A few days after he explained to me more fully the nature of his claim, and how he had been trifled with by Congress. I asked him his reasons for engaging in the American service; he told me that at the commencement of the war, the Big Knives (meaning the Americans), had advised him to turn his heart from the English, and promised to supply all his wants; and, as an additional inducement, that they would pay a better price for a scalp than had been usually given, and at the close of the war he should have land and stock sufficient to maintain himself and family: but he was now convinced they only meant to serve themselves, as he had frequently applied for a performance of their promises without success; and that he was determined to get satisfaction some way or other.

I told him I was not not sorry for his disappointments; that he was a bad Indian for deserting his good father, who lived on the other side the great water, and who was universally beloved by all who knew him, particularly by the Loretto nation; and as the subjects of this great and good father lived near his village, and gave every proof of their love and friendship to his nation, which he could not be ignorant of, I was surprized that he should suffer his heart to be moved by the changeable winds, and was sorry to add, that I believed he was the only Loretto Indian with two minds, and therefore I was unwilling to say any thing in his behalf before Congress.

These remarks on his conduct seemed to affect him, and he replied, that he hoped, notwithstanding he had deserted the cause of his great father, he should find me his friend to attend him when his affair should be taken under consideration by Congress, as he had not any one in New York who could serve him so essentially. I told him, that in spite of my just displeasure, his situation had melted my heart, and I would not refuse his request.

In about four days he came to acquaint me that Congress were then sitting, and he believed they would pay his demand if I would go with him, and interpret to the governor; but having taken an active part against the Americans during the war, I would willingly have been excused. On his urging my promise to him, I could not resist, and immediately accompanied him to the council, where Governor Franklin was president, who asked me if I knew Indian John; I told him, only by seeing him at New York, and that I came at his particular request to speak in his behalf. He desired me to assure the Indian that he might depend on having his demand satisfied in a few days, and to make his mind easy: this I communicated to him, with which he seemed perfectly satisfied.

Soon after he was sent for, and he received an order on a merchant for one hundred dollars, which being presented for payment, was not honoured: this incensed John, and he desired me to tell the merchant, that the Congress and their agents were all thieves. The merchant excused himself by saying that the treasury was very poor, and could not immediately satisfy every demand.

The next day John went again to the governor, and having acquainted him with the refusal of the draft, received an order on another merchant, which was duly honoured. John's heart was quite elated, and in less than ten days he had disposed of all the money, like a true Indian, principally in drink.

My interference in favour of the Indian made me well known, and procured me an introduction to a respectable mercantile house, from which I got credit for the Indian trade. Having arranged my cargo, I proceeded in a vessel to Albany, where I arrived on the 18th of June.

At this place I unloaded my goods, and got them conveyed in a waggon to Schenectady, where I purchased two boats. On the 6th of July I proceeded up the Mohawk River, to the German Flats, where I stayed three days; during which time a band of Oneida Indians came and solicited me to winter at their village, which was about ten days march from Fort Stanwix. I complied with their request, and set off with twenty-eight horses to carry my baggage, being obliged to travel through the woods, and sold my boats to satisfy those from whom I hired the horses. I arrived safe at the village with all my goods, but finding the plan was not likely to turn out advantageous, after a residence with them three weeks, I bartered for the few skins they had, and having re-purchased my boats, I left my Indian friends, proceeding immediately to the Jenesee Lake, where I arrived on the 14th of September.

Having landed and secured my goods, I ordered my men to prepare a house. The chiefs, on hearing of my arrival, assembled, and came up to me, accompanied by their young men, expecting presents, which I was obliged to make; and I asked permission to stay on their ground. Some consented, and others disapproved; at the last, after consulting each other, they told me I might go on with the building. The men immediately proceeded with cheerfulness and dispatch, in hopes of finishing the business before their return; but how transitory are all human events! whilst the men were at work, some Indians came in great haste to desire my attendance at the council fire, which was at a small distance from my intended place of residence. I obeyed the summons, and sat down by the chiefs, when one of them rose up, and addressed me to the following effect.

"You are the Sugar, for so you are called in our tongue, but you must not have too much sweetness on your lips. All the Oneida Indians say they have heard that you are only come under a pretence to get our lands from us; but this must not be, my young warriors will not suffer any Englishman to settle here. You are like the great chief, General Johnson, who asked for a spot of ground, or large bed, to lie on; and when Hendrick, the chief of the Mohawks, had granted his request, he got possession of a great quantity of our hunting grounds; and we have reason to think that you intend to dream us out of our natural rights. We loved Sir William, and therefore consented to all his requests; but you are a stranger, and must not take these liberties: therefore, my advice is, that you depart to-morrow at break of day, or you will be plundered by the young warriors, and it will not be in our power to redress you."

As I have mentioned a council, I shall describe the form of a house erected for that purpose near Fort Pitt.

The building is long, with two fires in it at a proper distance from each other, without any chimney or partition: the entry into the house is by two doors, one at each end: over the door the figure of a turtle was drawn, which is the ensign of the particular tribe: on each doorpost was cut out the face of an old man, an emblem of that gravity and wisdom that every senator ought to be possessed of. On each side, the whole length of the house within, is a platform, or bed, five feet wide, raised above the floor one foot and a half, made of broad pieces of wood split, which serves equally for a bed to sleep on, and a place to sit down. It is covered with a handsome mat made of rushes, and at the upper end of the building the king, or great chief sat.

To return from this digression,—We baled up our goods, and proceeded to Fort Oswego, which I attempted to pass, but was prevented by a centinel, who informed me that no batteau with goods could pass without the commanding officer's permission. I told him I was not an American, and would wait on him to know if he had issued such orders. I travelled in my Indian dress, and left my men at the landing, about a mile and a half from the garrison. I paid my respects to him, and acquainted him with my situation: he told me he should be very happy to oblige me, but that it was impossible to pass the fort without proper credentials; and as I had them not, he desired me to return to the United States, to prevent my goods being seized. Notwithstanding this friendly advice, I was determined to run the risk, and, to my extreme mortification, they were all seized by the custom-house officers, by them deposited in the king's warehouse, and afterwards condemned.

In this distressed situation, and very ill in health, I went down in a king's boat to Cataraqui, where I arrived on the 8th of November, and took up my abode at Mr. Howell's tavern. My indisposition increasing, I was obliged to keep to my blankets, and had only one faithful squaw to attend me. In this miserable state I lay some time, expecting every hour to change my climate, though determined to use every endeavour to effect a recovery. At this interesting period my correspondent arrived from England, and notwithstanding the losses he had sustained by my imprudence, performed the part of a good Samaritan, pouring oil and wine into my wounds; and finding my disorder required medical assistance, desired a surgeon to attend me, and I was soon sufficiently recovered to pursue my journey to La Chine, where I remained some months in preparing the goods which he brought from England for a North-west journey among the Indians, intending to go next spring to Michillimakinac; *mais la mauvaise fortune qui nous poursuivit toûjours*, frustrated all our schemes, and obliged us to leave La Chine on the 26th of May, 1786, from whence we proceeded in a large Schenectady boat to Oswegatche, where we stopped a few hours, and landed at a place called Toniata Creek, where I determined to apply for five hundred acres of land as a loyalist settler; which being granted me by government, I immediately felled timber to build a house for the accommodation of Indians, in hopes of deriving considerable advantages by barter.

In a few days the Indians came to trade with us, which gave us encouragement, and at the same time flattered us with the pleasing ideas of succeeding in commerce: but some affairs requiring my friend's attendance at Montreal, trade suffered a temporary suspense, and at his return he told me that we must leave our quarters, for he was apprehensive of a seizure for an English debt.

In this cruel dilemma, flight was our only security, and we embarked all our goods on board a large batteau, and proceeded to Pimitiscotyan, landing upon Lake Ontario, where we entered a creek, and found accommodation at a trader's house. The next morning we prepared a house for trade, and for some days went on successfully; but our happiness was of short duration, for an officer pursued us, and took possession of all the effects he could find, even to the tent which sheltered us from the weather, and carried them down to Montreal, where they were sold for less than one fourth part of their original cost and charges.— Thus circumstanced, without any property to trade with, we came down to the Bay of Kenty, and resided there ten months among the loyalist settlers, whose hospitality tended to soften the rigour of distress, and alleviate my sorrows. Early in spring, 1786, we crossed over to Carlton Island, and from thence to Fort Oswego, intending to go into the United States by that post; but not having any pass, we were not allowed to pursue our journey. In this mortifying situation I advised my friend to adopt another plan, and procured a conveyance to Salmon Creek, about twenty miles from the Fort. Here we rested one day, and with five pounds of pork, and two loaves of bread, we set off on foot, escorted by a squaw, expecting to reach Fort Stanwix in about four days; but the old path was entirely obliterated, and we were obliged to return in the evening to the creek, disappointed in the attempt. Unwilling to make another effort, we agreed to return to Fort Oswego, and though the distance was not more than twenty miles, we were six days before we reached the garrison.

In this expedition my friend suffered great hardships, not being accustomed to sleep in the woods; and having also a knapsack with about thirty pounds weight to carry, grieved him exceedingly: the shortness of provisions increased the distress, for it cannot be supposed that five pounds of pork, and two loaves of bread, would last three persons any length of time.

Previous to our journey's end, we were twelve hours without any sustenance, except wild onions; but fortunately we found on the sand about one hundred and forty birds eggs, which we boiled, and eagerly devoured, notwithstanding the greatest part had young birds in them, with small down on their bodies.

On our arrival at the fort, the commanding officer rallied us on our attempt; and taking my friend aside, advised him either to return to Montreal, or go up to Niagara, as he was sure he was not equal to the fatigue of an Indian life. He followed the officer's advice, and left me at the fort, which I soon afterwards quitted, and went down to Montreal; from thence I got a conveyance to Quebec; and being greatly distressed, applied to Lord Dorchester for relief, who generously directed his aid de camp to accompany me to Lieut. General Hope, and strongly recommended me to his notice, to be employed in an Indian capacity. Being in some measure relieved, and supplied with a few dollars and other necessaries, I was sent up to Cataraqui.

I left Quebec, and arrived at Montreal on the 14th of July: the next day I pursued my journey on foot, but seeing two Indians of my acquaintance in a canoe, and having some money in my pocket to buy rum, I hired them to convey me to Cataraqui, and in our way we killed plenty of game.

On the 19th of August I delivered my credentials to the proper officer, but he could not render me any service; however, he recommended me, by letter, to his friend at Carlton Island, where Sir John Johnson was waiting for a vessel to convey him to Niagara, to hold a council with the Indians: fortunately I procured an interview with him, and communicating to him my situation, he ordered me to be in readiness to assist as interpreter at his return. On the 18th of September, Sir John Johnson met us at the head of the bay of Kenty; the instant the Indians heard of his arrival, they saluted him with a discharge of small arms, and having received some rum, they danced and sung all night their war songs; one of them I particularly noticed, which was to the following effect :—

" At last our good father is arrived, he has broken the small branches, " and cleared his way to meet us. He has given us presents in abun-" dance, and only demands this large bed (meaning a considerable tract " of land which was described on a map)."

At twelve o'clock the next day a council was held, and Sir John laid his map before them, desiring a tract of land from Toronto to Lake Huron. This the Indians agreed to grant him, and the deed of gift being shewn them, it was signed by the chiefs' affixing the emblem, or figure of their respective totams, as their signatures.

Sir John Johnson then left them, and embarked for Cataraqui, the capital of the loyalist settlements.

Previous to his departure, I made him more fully acquainted with my distressed situation, and procured from him a temporary supply, which enabled me to go down to the third Township in the Bay of Kenty, where I stayed with my loyalist friends till the spring of 1787; during which time I had frequent opportunities of making observations on the flourishing state of the new settlements.

The settlements of loyalists in Canada, bid fair to be a valuable acquisition to Great Britain ; and in case of a war with the United States, will be able to furnish not only some thousands of veteran troops, but a rising generation of a hardy race of men, whose principles during the last war stimulated them to every exertion, even at the expence of their property, family, and friends, in support of the cause they so warmly espoused. There was, however, when I resided in the country, one cause of complaint, which, though it may not immediately affect the welfare and prosperity of the present inhabitants, or prevent an encrease of population, in proportion to the unlocated lands, is big with impending danger, and which, for the satisfaction of the public, I shall endeavour to explain.

All the land from Point au Baudet (the beginning of the loyalist settlements on the River St. Laurence), to the head of the bay of Kenty, which at this period I am informed, contains at least ten thousand souls, is said to be liable to the old feudal system of the French seigneuries; the lords of which claim title to receive some rent, or exercise some paramount right, which, though it may be at present very insignificant, and which perhaps may never be insisted on, renders every man dependent on the lord of the manor, and, in process of time, as land becomes more valuable, the raising these rents, or the exercise of these rights, may occasion frequent disputes: I think therefore, with submission to our government, that as many hundreds of Americans are now settled there, and doubtless many more may occasionally migrate from the United States, either from being disgusted with the polity of the country, or from an idea of reaping greater benefits as subjects of Great Britain, it behoves us to remove every obstacle of subserviency, and either by purchase, or any other mode Administration shall think fit to adopt, render all the lands in Canada, granted to loyalist subjects, or others who have, or may voluntarily take the oaths of allegiance, as free as those in Nova Scotia.

Men who have been engaged in their country's cause from the best of principles, should have every possible indulgence; and in proportion as they have been deprived of comforts by the desolation of war, they should be recompensed without any partial restrictions, and the remainder of their days rendered as happy as the government they live under can make them.

The population of these new settlements, and their parallel situation with Fort Oswegatche, Carleton Island, Oswego, and Niagra, evince, perhaps, more forcibly than ever, the propriety of retaining these barriers in our possession, which, in the former part of this work, I have fully explained; and as the third Township alone (which is nine miles square) contained, in the year 1787, about seventeen hundred inhabitants, it is difficult to say what number of valuable subjects that country may hereafter produce; certain it is, that it is capable of supporting multitudes, as the land is in general fertile, and on an average produces about thirty bushels of wheat per acre, even in the imperfect manner in which it is cleared, leaving all the stumps about three feet high, and from five to ten trees on an acre. This mode of clearing is in fact absolutely necessary, because new cultivated lands in hot climates require shelter, to prevent the scorching heat of the sun, which, in its full power, would burn up the seed. It has also been found expedient in stony ground to let the stones remain, as they retain a moisture favorable to vegetation.

In the month of May I left the new settlements, and went down to Montreal, and from thence to Quebec, where I waited on Lord Dorchester, but could not gain admittance. I was afterwards informed that his lordship was indisposed. I then went to Lieut General Hope's, but he had embarked for England.

So many mortifying disappointments affected me very sensibly, but as discouragements generally encreased my exertions, I was more assiduous in my endeavours to live, and whilst I was contriving schemes for future support, I received a supply from a friend: so seasonable a relief braced up all my nerves, and I felt a pleasure that can scarce be conceived by any but such as have experienced hardships and difficulties similar to mine.

My heart being cheered, and every gloomy thought dispersed, I determined to leave the country whilst I had money in my pocket. Having found another friend to sign a pass, I went on board a ship then lying in the River St. Laurence, on the 25th of October, and arrived in London the beginning of December following, rejoiced at again setting foot on my native shore.

Having finished the historical part of my work, I have only to solicit the candid indulgence of the public for any literary errors I may have been guilty of; and with great respect to convey to them an humble hope that the Voyages and Travels, together with the Vocabulary subjoined, may not be found totally unworthy their attention.

VOCABULARY.

English.	Esquimeaux.
Arrow	Kátso
Bow	Petíksick
Boat	Kágak
Dog	Mické, or Tímitok
Eye	Killick, or Shik
Egg	Manneguk
Ear	Tehiu
Four (number)	Missílagat
Foot	Itikak
Hair	Nutshad
Heaven	Taktuck, or Nabugákshe
Head	Níakock
Knife	Shavić
Moon	Tákock
Oar	Pácotick
One (number)	Kombuc
Sun	Shíkonac, or Sakáknuc
Two (number)	Tigal
Three (number)	Ké
Rain	Kíllaluck
Tooth	Ukak
Water	Sillakákto

N. B. *Esquimeau, in the singular Number, means an Eater of raw Flesh.*

VOCABULARY.

English.	Iroquois.
One	Uskat
Two	Tekkeny
Three	Aghsey
Four	Kayeery
Five	Wisk
Six	Yàyak
Seven	Tsyàdak
Eight	Sadégo
Nine	Tyoughtow
Ten	Oyéry
Eleven	Oyéry uskat yawàrey
Twelve	Oyéry tekkeny yawàrey
Thirteen	Oyéry aghsey yawàrey
Fourteen	Oyéry kayeery yawàrey
Fifteen	Oyéry wisk yawàrey
Sixteen	Oyéry yàyak yawàrey
Seventeen	Oyéry tsyàdak yawàrey
Eighteen	Oyéry sadégo yawàrcy
Nineteen	Oyéry tyoughtow yawàrey
Twenty	Towwaghsey
Twenty one	Towwaghsey uskat yawàrey
Twenty two	Towwaghsey tekkeny yawàrey
Twenty three	Towwaghsey aghsey yawàrey
Twenty four	Towwaghsey kayeery yawàrey
Twenty five	Towwaghsey wisk yawàrey

VOCABULARY.

Algonkin.	*Chippeway.*
Payjik	Payshik
Ninch	Neesh
Nissoo	Neesswoy
Neoo	Neon
Naran	Narnan
Ningootwassoo	Negutwosswoy
Ninchowassoo	Neeshswosswoy
Nissowassoo	Swosswoy
Shongassoo	Shangosswoy
Metassoo	Metosswoy
Metassoo ashy payjik	Metosswoy asshea payshik
Metassoo ashy ninch	Metosswoy asshea neesh
Metassoo ashy nissoo	Metosswoy asshea neesswoy
Metassoo ashy neoo	Metosswoy asshea neon
Metassoo ashy naran	Metosswoy asshea narnan
Metassoo ashy ningootwassoo	Metosswoy asshea negutwosswoy
Metassoo ashy ninchowassoo	Metosswoy asshea neeshswosswoy
Metassoo ashy nissowassoo	Metosswoy asshea swosswoy
Metassoo ashy shongassoo	Metosswoy asshea shangosswoy
Ninchtànà	Neesh tanner
Ninchtànà ashy payjik	Neesh tanner asshea payshik
Ninchtànà ashy ninch	Neesh tanner asshea neesh
Ninchtànà ashy nissoo	Neesh tanner asshea neesswoy
Ninchtànà ashy neoo	Neesh tanner asshea neon
Ninchtànà ashy naran	Neesh tanner asshea narnan

VOCABULARY.

English.	Iroquois.
Twenty six	Towwaghsey yàyak yawàrey
Twenty seven	Towwaghsey tsyàdak yawàrey
Twenty eight	Towwaghsey sadégo yawàrey
Twenty nine	Towwaghsey tyoughtow yawàrey
Thirty	Aghscy newaghsey
Thirty one	Aghscy newaghsey uskat yawàrey
Thirty two	Aghsey newaghsey tekkeny yawàrey
Thirty three	Aghscy newaghsey aghscy yawàrey
Thirty four	Aghsey newaghsey kayeery yawàrey
Thirty five	Aghsey newaghsey wisk yawàrey
Thirty six	Aghsey newaghsey yàyak yawàrey
Thirty seven	Aghsey newaghsey tsyàdak yawàrey
Thirty eight	Aghsey newaghsey sadégo yawàrey
Thirty nine	Aghsey newaghsey tyoughtow yawàrey
Forty	Kayeery newaghsey
Forty one	Kayeery newaghscy uskat yawàrey
Forty two	Kayeery newaghscy tekkeny yawàrey
Forty three	Kayeery newaghsey aghscy yawàrey
Forty four	Kayeery newaghscy kaycery yawàrey
Forty five	Kayeery newaghsey wisk yawàrey
Forty six	Kayeery newaghscy yàyak yawàrey

VOCABULARY.

Algonkin.	*Chippeway.*
Ninchtànà ashy ningootwassoo	Neesh tanner asshea negutwosswoy
Ninchtànà ashy ninchowassoo	Neesh tanner asshea neeshswosswoy
Ninchtànà ashy nissowassoo	Neesh tanner asshea swosswoy
Ninchtànà ashy shongassoo	Neesh tanner asshea shangosswoy
Nisso metànà	Neess semmettenner
Nissoo metànà ashy payjik	Neess semmettenner asshea payshik
Nissoo metànà ashy ninch	Neess semmettenner asshea neesh
Nissoo metànà ashy nissoo	Neess semmettenner asshea neesswoy
Nissoo metànà ashy neoo	Neess semmettenner asshea neon
Nissoo metànà ashy naran	Neess semmettenner asshea narnan
Nissoo metànà ashy ningootwassoo	Neess semmettenner asshea negutwosswoy
Nissoo metànà ashy ninchowassoo	Neess semmettenner asshea neeshswosswoy
Nissoo metànà ashy nissowassoo	Neess semmettenner asshea swosswoy
Nissoo metànà ashy shongassoo	Neess semmettenner asshea shangosswoy
Neoo metànà	Neon mettenner
Neoo metànà ashy payjik	Neon mettenner asshea payshik
Neoo metànà ashy ninch	Neon mettenner asshea neesh
Neoo metànà ashy nissoo	Neon mettenner asshea neesswoy
Neoo metànà ashy neoo	Neon mettenner asshea neon
Neoo metànà ashy naran	Neon mettenner asshea narnan
Neoo metànà ashy ningootwassoo	Neon mettenner asshea negutwosswoy

VOCABULARY.

English.	Iroquois.
Forty seven	Kayeery newaghsey tsyàdak yawàrey
Forty eight	Kayeery newaghsey sadégo yawàrey
Forty nine	Kayeery newaghsey tyoughtow yawàrey
Fifty	Wisk newaghsey
Fifty one	Wisk newaghscy uskat yawàrey
Fifty two	Wisk newaghsey tekkeny yawàrey
Fifty three	Wisk newaghsey aghsey yawàrey
Fifty four	Wisk newaghsey kayeery yawàrey
Fifty five	Wisk newaghsey wisk yawàrey
Fifty six	Wisk newaghsey yàyak yawàrey
Fifty seven	Wisk newaghsey tsyàdak yawàrey
Fifty eight	Wisk newaghsey sadégo yawàrey
Fifty nine	Wisk newaghsey tyoughtow yawàrey
Sixty	Yàyak newaghsey
Sixty one	Yàyak newaghsey uskat yawàrey
Sixty two	Yàyak newaghsey tekkeny yawàrey
Sixty three	Yàyak newaghsey aghsey yawàrey
Sixty four	Yàyak newaghsey kayeery yawàrey
Sixty five	Yàyak newaghsey wisk yawàrey

VOCABULARY.

Algonkin.	Chippeway.
Neoo metànà ashy ninchowassoo	Neon mettenner asshea neeshswoswoy
Neoo metànà ashy nissowassoo	Neon mettenner asshea swosswoy
Neoo metànà ashy shongassoo	Neon mettenner asshea shangosswoy
Naran metànà	Nar mettenner
Naran metànà ashy payjik	Nar mettenner asshea payshik
Naran metànà ashy ninch	Nar mettenner asshea neesh
Naran metànà ashy nissoo	Nar mettenner asshea neesswoy
Naran metànà ashy neoo	Nar mettenner asshea neon
Naran metànà ashy naran	Nar mettenner asshea narnan
Naran metànà ashy ningootwassoo	Nar mettenner asshea negutwosswoy
Naran metànà ashy ninchowassoo	Nar mettenner asshea neeshswosswoy
Naran metànà ashy nissowassoo	Nar mettenner asshea swosswoy
Naran metànà ashy shongassoo	Nar mettenner asshea shangosswoy
Ningootwassoo metànà	Negutwoss semmettenner
Ningootwassoo metànà ashy payjik	Negutwoss semmettenner asshea payshik
Ningootwassoo metànà ashy ninch	Negutwoss semmettenner asshea neesh
Ningootwassoo metànà ashy nissoo	Negutwoss semmettenner asshea neesswoy
Ningootwassoo metànà ashy neoo	Negutwoss semmettenner asshea neon
Ningootwassoo metànà ashy naran	Negutwoss semmettenner asshea narnan

VOCABULARY.

English.	Iroquois.
Sixty six	Yàyak newaghsey yàyak yawàrey
Sixty seven	Yàyak newaghsey tsyàdak yawàrey
Sixty eight	Yàyak newaghsey sadégo yawàrey
Sixty nine	Yàyak newaghsey tyoughtow yawàrey
Seventy	Tsyàdak newaghsey
Seventy one	Tsyàdak newaghsey uskat yawàrey
Seventy two	Tsyàdak newaghsey tekkeny yawàrey
Seventy three	Tsyàdak newaghsey aghsey yawàrey
Seventy four	Tsyàdak newaghsey kayeery yawàrey
Seventy five	Tsyàdak newagsey wisk yawàrey
Seventy six	Tsyàdak newaghsey yàyak yawàrey
Seventy seven	Tsyàdak newaghsey tsyàdak yawàrey
Seventy eight	Tsyàdak newaghsey sadégo yawàrey
Seventy nine	Tsyàdak newaghsey tyoughtow yawàrey

VOCABULARY.

Algonkin.	Chippeway.
Ningootwassoo metànà ashy ningootwassoo	Negutwoss semmettenner asshea negutwosswoy
Ningootwassoo metànà ashy ninchowassoo	Negutwoss semmettenner asshea neeshswosswoy
Ningootwassoo metànà ashy nissowassoo	Negutwoss semmettenner asshea swosswoy
Ningootwassoo metànà ashy shongassoo	Negutwoss semmettenner asshea shangosswoy
Ninchowassoo metànà	Neeshswoss semmettenner
Ninchowassoo metànà ashy payjik	Neeshswoss semmettenner asshea payshik
Ninchowassoo metànà ashy ninch	Neeshswoss semmettenner asshea neesh
Ninchowassoo metànà ashy nissoo	Neeshswoss semmettenner asshea neesswoy
Ninchowassoo metànà ashy neoo	Neeshswoss semmettenner asshea neon
Ninchowassoo metànà ashy naran	Neeshswoss semmettenner asshea narnan
Ninchowassoo' metànà ashy ningootwassoo	Neeshswoss semmettenner asshea negutwosswoy
Ninchowassoo metànà ashy ninchowassoo	Neeshswoss semmettenner asshea neeshswosswoy
Ninchowassoo metànà ashy nissowassoo	Neeshswoss semmettenner asshea swosswoy
Ninchowassoo metànà ashy shongassoo	Neeshswoss semmettenner asshea shangosswoy

VOCABULARY.

English.	Iroquois.
Eighty	Sadégo newaghsey
Eighty one	Sadégo newaghsey uskat yawàrey
Eighty two	Sadégo newaghsey tekkeny yawàrey
Eighty three	Sadégo newaghsey aghsey yawàrey
Eighty four	Sadégo newaghscy kayeery yawàrey
Eighty five	Sadégo newaghsey wisk yawàrey
Eighty six	Sadégo newaghsey yàyak yawàrey
Eighty seven	Sadégo newaghsey tsyàdak yawàrey
Eighty eight	Sadégo newaghsey sadégo yawàrey
Eighty nine	Sadégo newaghsey tyoughtow yawàrey
Ninety	Tyoughtow newaghsey
Ninety one	Tyoughtow newaghsey uskat yawàrey
Ninety two	Tyoughtow newaghsey tekkeny yawàrey
Ninety three	Tyoughtow newaghsey aghsey yawàrey
Ninety four	Tyoughtow newaghsey kayeery yawàrey
Ninety five	Tyoughtow newaghsey wisk yawàrey
Ninety six	Tyoughtow newaghsey yàyak yawàrey

VOCABULARY.

Algonkin.	Chippeway.
Nissowassoo metànà	Swoss semmettenner
Nissowassoo metànà ashy payjik	Swoss semmettenner asshea payshik
Nissowassoo metànà ashy ninch	Swoss semmettenner asshea neesh
Nissowassoo metànà ashy nissoo	Swoss semmettenner asshea neesswoy
Nissowassoo metànà ashy neoo	Swoss semmettenner ashea neon
Nissowassoo metànà ashy naran	Swoss semmettenner asshea narnan
Nissowassoo metànà ashy ningootwassoo	Swoss semmettenner asshea negatwosswoy
Nissowassoo metànà ashy ninchowassoo	Swoss semmettenner asshea neeshswosswoy
Nissowassoo metànà ashy nissowassoo	Swoss semmettenner asshea swosswoy
Nissowassoo metànà ashy shongassoo	Swoss semmettenner asshea shangosswoy
Shongassoo metànà	Shangoss semmettenner
Shongassoo metànà ashy payjik	Shangoss semmettenner asshea payshik
Shongassoo metànà ashy ninch	Shangoss semmettenner asshea neesh
Shongassoo metànà ashy nissoo	Shangoss semmettenner asshea neesswoy
Shongassoo metànà ashy neoo	Shangoss semmettenner asshea neon
Shongassoo metànà ashy naran	Shangoss semmettenner asshea narnan
Shongassoo metànà ashy ningootwassoo	Shangoss semmettenner asshea negutwosswoy

C c

VOCABULARY.

English.	Iroquois.
Ninety seven	Tyoughtow newaghsey tsyàdak yawàrey
Ninety eight	Tyoughtow newaghsey sadégo yawàrey
Ninety nine	Tyoughtow newaghsey tyoughtow yawàrey
One hundred	Uskat towaneyow
Two hundred	Tekkeny towaneyow
Three hundred	Aghsey towaneyow
Four hundred	Kaycery towaneyow
Five hundred	Wisk towaneyow
Six hundred	Yàyak towaneyow
Seven hundred	Tsyàdak towaneyow
Eight hundred	Sadégo towaneyow
Nine hundred	Tyoughtow towancyow
One thousand	Oyéry towaneyow

VOCABULARY.

Algonkin.	Chippeway.
Shongassoo metànà ashy ninchowassoo	Shangoss semmettenner asshea neeshswosswoy
Shongassoo metànà ashy nissowassoo	Shangoss semmettenner asshea swosswoy
Shongassoo metànà ashy shongassoo	Shangoss semmettenner asshea shangosswoy
Metassoo metànà	Negut wauk
Metassoo ninchtànà metànà	Neesh wauk
Metassoo nissoo metànà	Neesswoy wauk
Metassoo neoo metànà	Neon wauk
Metassoo naran metànà	Nar wauk
Metassoo ningootwassoo metànà	Negutwoss wauk
Metassoo ninchowasso metànà	Neeshswoss wauk
Metassoo nissowassoo metànà	Swoss wauk
Metassoo shongassoo metànà	Shangoss wauk
Metassoo metassoo metànà	Metosswoy kitchee wauk

A TABLE OF WORDS

Shewing, in a variety of Instances, the Difference as well as Analogy between the Algonkin and Chippeway Languages, with the English Explanation.

English.	Algonkin.	Chippeway.
To abandon, or forsake	Packiton	Packitan
To arrive at a place	Takouchin	Takooshin
To assist	Mawinewah	Mawinewah
To alter, or change	Miscoush	Mishcoot
To amuse, or play	Packeguay	Athtergain
To beat, or bruise	Packité	Packettywaun
To believe	Tilerimah, or tikerimah	Indenendum gwoyack
To be willing	Wisch	Cannar, or cunner
To call	Tychintkaw	Nandootum
To carry	Petou, or peta	Keemarjemet
To dance	Nemeh	Nemeh
To do, or make	Toshiton	Ojeytoon, or Tojeytoon

VOCABULARY.

English.	Algonkin.	Chippeway.
To dwell, or stay	Tapia	Appay
To drink	Minikwah	Minniquah
To eat	Wissin	Wissinnin
To freeze	Kissim	Mushcowwartin
To fall	Ponkisin	Ponkissin
To find	Nantounewaw	Warbermeco
To go by water	Pimmiscaw	Pamiskian, or pemiskar
To go by land	Teja	Papamôtay
To give	Millaw	Darmissey
To govern	Tibarimaw	Tibarimaw
To have	Tindala	Arwayyor
To hunt	Keoussey	Geosay
To hate	Shinguerimaw	Nesharquish
To keep	Ganawerimaw	Gannewainnemar
To kill	Nesa	Gunnesar
To know	Kekerindan	Keecannawendan
To love, or love	Sakiar	Zargay, or zargeytoon
To lose	Packilague	Winnetoon
To laugh	Kapy	Pawpy
To lie down	Weepemaw	Neparhan
To meet	Nantoonewar	Ncewatch

VOCABULARY.

English.	Algonkin.	Chippeway.
To marry	Weewin	Tuckunnumkewish
To make water	Minsy	Meesesay
To make fire, & cook	Pootawee	Pooterway chebockwoy
To pay	Tipaham	Guddyparhan
To please	Mirowerrindan	Mirrowerrindan
To perspire	Matootoo	Matootoo
To run	Pitcheba	Squamich
To row	Pimisca	Pemishkar
To sit down	Mantippy	Mantetappy
To seek	Nantawerima	Warcharch
To sing	Sheshin	Najemoon
To steal	Kemootin	Keemôtyan
To sleep	Nepa	Nepan
To smoke a pipe	Saggasoy	Suggersoy
To speak	Galoola	Debarchim, or debarchemon
To see	Wabemo	Wabemat, or wabemor
To take	Takoonan	Tarpenan
To think	Tilelindan	Indenendum, or indenind
To tell	Teta	Gudjey
To throw away, or repudiate	Webenan	Waybenan

VOCABULARY.

English.	Algonkin.	Chippeway.
To understand	Nistotawa	Neesstootewar
To vex	Iskatissey	Annascartissey, or nishcartissey
To walk, or go	Pemousse	Pamôsay
To win	Packitan	Warmatt

Axe	Ajackwet	Ajackquoit
Above, or high	Spimink	Ishpemeg
After, or afterwards	Mipidach	Ningoot
And	Gaye, or mipigaye	Ashea
Another	Coutak	Ningootch
Again, or yet	Menawatch	Meenewatch
All	Kakina	Cockinnor
Always, wherever	Kakeli	Cargoneek, or memarmo
Breech clout	Kepokitty kousah	Oncean
Beard	Mischiton	Opeewyesky
Barrel	Ayoentagun	Owentagun
Ball, or large shot	Alwin	Kitchee anwin
Bottle	Sheshegouay	Môtay
Beaver	Amik	Amik
Beaver skin	Appiminiquy	Appiminiquy
Body	Yao	Yoe

VOCABULARY.

English.	Algonkin.	Chippeway.
Blankets	Wabiwyan	Waperwoyan
Breech	Miskousah	Peckqueen dorsow
Bear	Mackquah	Mackquah
Bear cub	Makons	Mackconce, or Mackquaconce
Bread, or flour	Paboushikan	Pockquoisigan
Broth, or soup	Wabou	Shoanarboop
Bag	Maskimout	Muchcomat
Blood	Miskoo	Misquy
Bark bowl, or cup	Oulagan	Onagun
Belly	Mishemout	Ishquamach
Brother	Necanish	Shemayn
Bowels	Olakick	Onuggesh
Birds, or fowl	Pilé	Pinneyshis
Because	Mewinch	Mewinch
Black	Negao	Mackcutty
Big	Mentitoo	Menditoo
Coats	Capotewian	Piskawagan
Canoe	Cheeman	Cheeman
Companion, or friend	Neechee	Neejee, or Neecarnis
Captain, or chief	Okemaw	Okemaw, or Ojemaw
Captain, or head warrior	Kitchee okemaw semauganish	Kitchee Okemaw
Child, or children	Bobeloshin	Queebesince
Courage	Taquamissi	Taguamissy, or Haguamissy

VOCABULARY.

English.	Algonkin.	Chippeway.
Covetous	Sasakissy	Sazargesay
Cold	Kekatch	Geessennar
Duck, wild	Sheeship	Sheeshib
Dust	Pingway	Pingo
Deer	Awaskesh	Awaskesh
Dog	Alim	Anim
Dog, puppy	Alimons	Animonce
Day, or days	Okonogat	Ogunnegat
Dart	Sheshikwee	Aysquish
Dish	Mackoan	Mackoan
Dead	Neepoo	Neepoo
Devil, or Bad Spirit	Matchee Mannitoo	Matchee Mannitoo
Dance of Savages	Sheshequoy	Shessaquoy
Drunk	Ousqibby	Squibby, or Osquibby
Done, it is done, or past	Sheyar	Shyyar
Elk	Mons	Moouse
Eye	Ouskinshik	Wiskinky
English	Outsakamink dachereni	Saggonash
Equal	Tabiscooch	Tabiscoach
Each	Paypayjik	Papayjit
Enough	Mimilie	Mee, or mimilic
Fire steel	Scoutykan	Squittycan, or Scotayean
Fire	Scoute	Scotay or squitty

D d

VOCABULARY.

English.	Algonkin.	Chippeway.
Fort	Wackaygan	Wakaygan
French	Mittigoush	Waymistergoash
Fish	Kickons	Kegonce
Fish, white	Attikamek	Artikkameg
Fox	Outagamy	Assinbo
Flesh of animals	Weass	Weass
Fork or prong stick	Nassawokwot	Cawmeek meteek
Father	Nooskay	Nocey
Fat, or he is fat	Pimete	Pimmethy
Female, or woman	Ickwer	Equoy
Full	Mooshquenay	Mooshquenay
Free, generous	Walatissy	Ajackquoy
Formerly	Peraweego	Maywisher
Far off	Watso	Awassa, or Awassa woyta
Girl	Ickwessens	Equoysince
Gun	Paskeysegan	Baskeyzegan
Grass	Myask	Nepish, or mejask
Grapes	Shoamin	Minneshish
God, or Great Spirit	Kitchee Mannitoo	Kitchee Mannitoo
Gunpowder	Pingo Mackate	Mackcutty, or Pingo Mackcutty
Good	Quelatch	Nishshishshin
House, or hut	Wikiwam	Wigwaum
Hair, human	Lissy	Lissy

VOCABULARY.

English.	Algonkin.	Chippeway.
Hair, of beasts	Pewall	Opeeway
Heaven, or the other world	Spiminkaquin	Pockcan worrockey, or pockan tunnockey
Hare	Wapoos	Wapoos
Husband, or master of weakness.	Napema	Nabaim
Head	Ousteooan	Eshtergoan
Heart	Mishewah	Oathty
Half	Nabal	Arbittar
Handsome	Sasayga	Sasayga
Home, or dwelling	Entayank	Ashemich
Hot	Akeeshattay	Geeshartay
Hungry	Packatay	Bocketty
Here	Akonda, or akomanda	Ashemich
How	Tany	Tawny
How much, or how many?	Tantasou, or tarnimilik?	Tawnymilik?
Indian corn	Metamin	Medarmin
Iron	Pewaby	Pewabick
Island	Minis	Minnesey
Indians	Ishinawbah	Nishinnorbay
Immediately	Webatch	Webatch
Idle, or lazy	Kittimy	Kittim
Knife	Mockoman	Mokoman
Knife, crooked	Coutagan	Wakeckuman

VOCABULARY.

English.	Algonkin.	Chippeway.
Kettle, or pot	Akikkons	Akeek
Land	Oustikan	Onjee
Looking glasses	Wabemo	Warbemoon
Lake	Kitchee Gammink	Sakiegan
Letter	Marseynaygan	Marseynaygan
Leggons, or stockings	Metass	Mittasse
Light (clear)	Vendao	Meesharquoit
Long since	Shashayay	Sharshyyar
Little, small, few	Wabeloosheins	Pongay, or hagushenonce
Man	Alisinape	Ninnee
Moon, or night light	Debikat Ikisy	Geezus
Mistress, or wife	Neremoossin	Mentimoye
Merchandise	Alokatchigan	Huncushigon, or Annacotchigon
Medicine	Maskikik	Maskikkee
Male	Nape	Ayarbey
Male deer, or stag	Mecheway	Ayarbey awaskesh
Much	Nebela	Nepewar, or gwotch
Needle to sew with	Shabounekan	Shaboonegun
Nose	Yatch	Yotch
News	Taypatchimoo, kan	Mergummegat
Night	Debbikat	Debbikat
Near, or nigh	Pechoowetch	Payshew

VOCABULARY.

English.	Algonkin.	Chippeway.
Now	Nongom	Nogome
Never	Kawicka	Cawwickca, or cassawickca
No	Ka	Cawween, or ka
Nothing	Kakaygoo	Kakaygo
Not yet	Kamasshy	Kamarchy
Otter	Nekeek	Nekeek
Old, he was old	Kewesheins	Keewaency
Portage, or carrying place	Cappatagan	Onuggemeg
People, or nation	Irenee	Nondajewot
Paddle, or small oar	Apway	Abboy
Pike, (a fish)	Kenonjay	Kenonjay
Peninsula	Minnissin	Minnissin
Peace	Pekah	Meecho
Partridge	Pilesiwee	Peenay
Pipe	Poygan	Opoygan
Quick	Welibik	Annacook
Ring, for the finger	Debelincheebeson	Zenzeebisson
Rice, wild	Malomin	Menomon
Road	Meekan	Meekan
Rum, or brandy	Scoutiwaboy	Squittywabo, or scotaywabo

VOCABULARY.

English.	Algonkin.	Chippeway.
Rain	Kemewan	Kimmeevan
River	Sepim	Seepee
Roots of trees	Oustikwees	Watappy
Robe of peltry	Ockola	Woygan, or oakonus
Red	Misquy	Misquoy, or misquitty
Shirt	Papakewean	Parbockerwoyan
Spoon	Mickwan	Tamickquoin
Sword, or great knife	Semagan	Kitchee mokoman
Sense, to have sense	Nebwacka	Annaboycassey
Star	Alan	Annunk
Sturgeon	Lamek	Onnemay
Sea, or unbounded lake	Agankitchee gammink	Kitchee gammink
Stone	Assin	Assin
Spirit	Mannitoo	Mannitoo
Sun, or great light	Keesis	Geesessey
Shoes (Indian)	Mackisin	Maukissin
Ship, or great canoe	Kitchee cheeman	Kitchee Naberquoin
Soldier, or warrior	Semaganis	Shemagonish
Smoke, or fire fog	Pentakoe	Keenarbittay
Summer, or spring	Merockamink	Menokemeg
Sick	Outineous	Aquoisee
Sad	Talissimy	Cushkendummerman
Strong	Mashkawa	Mushcowar

VOCABULARY.

English.	Algonkin.	Chippeway.
Teeth	Tebit	Weebit
To-morrow	Wabank	Warbunk
Tomahawk	Agackwetons	Warcockquoite
Tongue, human	Ooton	Ooton
Tobacco	Sayma	Assaymer
Tobacco pouch	Kaspetagun	Kispetawgun
Trees	Meteek	Meteek
There	Mandadiby	Woity, or awoity
Too much	Ozam	Ozome
Too little	Ozame mangis	Ozome pangay
Thank you	Meegwatch	Meegwotch
Truly	Keket	Kaygait
That	Manda	Maunder
Together	Mamawee	Marnio
Vermillion	Oulamar	Ozonnemon
Village	Oudenank	Narpoon
Water	Nepee	Nippee
Winter	Pepoon	Bebone
Wolf	Mahingan	Mahingan
Wine, or blood red broth	Shoemin aboo	Mishquoy shoanarboop
Wind	Loutin	Noetting
Woods	Nopemenk	Menopemeg
War	Nontobâly	Mecartay
Weary, or tired	Takoosy	Nowwendayshon

English.	Algonkin.	Chippeway.
Why	Tanientien	Cannatoo
Where	Ta	Aunday
Where is he? or where does he dwell?	Tanepy appy	Tannepy Appay
What is that? what? or what now?	Waneweenay?	Wàygonin?
Who is that?	Waneweenay mabo?	Hawaneeyau?
Whence	Tannepy	Tannepy
White	Waby	Warbishcar
Yellow	Wazzo	Jônia
Yes	Mi, or Minkooty	Angaymer, or Nangaymer
Yesterday	Pitchylaga	Pitchynargo

VOCABULARY.

English.	Mohegan.	Shawanee.
A bear	Mquoh	Mauquah
A beaver	Amisque	Amaquah
Eye	Hkeesque	Skesacoo
Ear	Towohque	Towacah
Fetch	Pautoh	Peatoloo
My grandfather	Nemoghhome	Nemasompethau
My grandmother	Nohhum	Nocumthau
My grandchild	Naughees	Noosthethau
He goes	Pumissoo	Pomthalo
A girl	Peesquausoo	Sqauthauthau
House	Weekumuhm	Weecuah
He (that man)	Uwoh	Welah
His head	Weensis	Weensch
His heart	Utoh	Otahch
Hair	Weghaukun	Welathoh
Her husband	Waughecheh	Wasecheh
His teeth	Wepeeton	Wepeetalee
I thank you	Wneeweh	Neauweh
My uncle	Nsees	Neeseethau
I	Neah	Nelah
Thou	Keah	Kelah
We	Neaunuh	Nelauweh
Ye	Keauwuh	Kelauweh
Water	Nbey	Nippee
Elder sister	Nmees	Nemeethau
River	Sepoo	Thepee

VOCABULARY.

English.	Mohegan.
Bear	Mquoh
Beaver	Amisque
Dead, he is dead	Nboo, or Neepoo
Devil, or Bad Spirit	Mtandou
Dress the kettle, (make a fire)	Pootouwah
Eyes	Ukeesquan
Fire	Stauw
Give it him	Meenuh
How	Tunch
House	Weekumuhm
Go, or walk	Pumisseh
Marry	Weeween
River	Sepoo
Shoes	Mkissin
The sun	Keesogh
Sit down	Mattipeh
Water	Nbey
Where	Tehah
Winter	Hpoon
Wood	Metooque

N. B. The e final is not sounded except in monosyllables.

VOCABULARY.

Algonkin.	Chippeway.
Mackquah	Mackquah
Amik	Amik
Nepoo	Neepoo
Matchee Mannitoo	Matchee Mannitoo
Poutwah	Pooterway Chebockwoy
Ouskinshik	Wiskinky
Scoute	Scotay or Squitty
Millaw	Darmissey
Tany	Tawny
Wikiwam	Wigwaum
Pemousse	Pamosây
Wewin	Tuckunnumkewish
Sepim	Seepee
Mackisin	Maukissin
Keesis	Geessesscy
Mantippy	Mantetappy
Nepee	Nippee
Ta	Aunday
Pepoon	Bebone
Meteek	Meteck

VOCABULARY.

English.	Iroquois.
Above	Aynegun
Absent	Yáckta ohárlogh
Abuse, to	Henryotaxa
Accept, to	Iáyner
Account, to	Sastáyricey
Accuse, to	Cúttergun
Add to	Cayéntuck
Admire, to	Sannagatcácktone
Advice	Sattayéntack
Adultery	Sáchequar
Afraid	Sáquoy
Afternoon	Nowwátone
Again	Ségo
Agree, to	Curywyyárley
Alike	Sadáyyouth
All	Aguágo
Ally	Lanóha
Alone	Yáckta oya
Always	Chetko
Amuse, to	Susqueeselon
Another	Oya
Answer, to	Sattróly
And	Noke
A, an, or the	Ne, ne
Bread	Kanádaro
Black	Agohoonsay

VOCABULARY.

English.	Iroquois.
Dear	Carnolelow
English	Cherrihunságat
Father	Luggoney
Gunpowder	Ogánra
Give me	Cassar
How much, or how many	Toneego
Jacob	Yárwek
King, or great chief	Sachem
Money	Wisstar
Montreal	Chocktyhargo
Or	Neteas
Partridge	Oquesses
Peter	Gwider
Plenty	Cúshcowait
Perhaps	Togatt
Rose (a flower)	Easel
Rum	Skarat

VOCABULARY.

English.	Iroquois.
Shot	Onáya
Sugar	Chekayter
Silver works	Wisstar noolone
Thank you	Yaown
There is	Honerer
Understand, to	Cockharonckar
Wise	Satoákha
Wind	Yowwetty
Win, to	Rowwennéhoo
Willing	Senooncy
Wild	Yáckta satoákha
Wife	Sannatella
White	Carárger
War	Satterleyhone
Who	Unghka
Was	Ne
Water	Oghnéga
Wine, or blood red soup	Onéahháradáschhoúhtscrákeri
Who was	Ungka ne
What was	Oghnihayadòtea
Where	Caha
Virgin	Hanághgwáyenden

VOCABULARY.

English.	Iroquois.
Young	Agúntelo
You	Ecee
Yesterday	Tyoúcktárlow
Yes	Etho
Yellow	Ajeenegwar
Year	Atoori
Your health	Honoroquennyee

Names of Furs and Skins in English and French.

English.	French.
Fat winter beaver	Castor gras d'hiver
Fat summer beaver	Castor gras d'été
Dry winter beaver	Castor secs d'hiver
Dry summer beaver	Castor secs d'été
Old winter beaver	Castor vieux d'hiver
Old summer beaver	Castor vieux d'été
Raw stage skins	Cerfs verts
Prepared stage skins	Cerfs passés
Rein deer skins	Caribous
Raw hind skins	Biches vertes
Prepared hind skins	Biches passées
Mush rats	Rats musques
Prepared roebuck skins	Chevreuils passés
Unprepared roebuck skins	Chevreuils verts
Tanned roebuck skins	Chevreuils tanés
Southern, or Virginia foxes	Renards du sud ou Virginie
White, from Tadousac, foxes	Renards blancs de Tadousac
Wolves	Loups de bois
Beaver eaters	Carcajous
Martens	Martres
Squirrels, black	Ecureuils, noirs
Squirrels, grey	Ecureuils, argentés

VOCABULARY.

English.	French.
Fishers	Peccans
Bears	Ours
Bears, Cub	Oursons
Otters	Loutres
Cats	Chats
Lynx	Loups cerviers
Foxes, red	Renards rouges
Foxes, cross	Renards croisés
Foxes, black	Renards noirs
Foxes, grey	Renards argentés
Minks	Visons, ou Fourtreaux
North Case Cat	Pichoux du nord
South Case Cat	Pichoux du sud

VOCABULARY.

Parts of the Human Body.

English.	Chippeway.
Ankle	Warwich
Arm	Aník
Arm, broken	Késconeek
Back	Oníckquick
Beard	Opeewyésky
Belly	Is'quamach
Blood	Misqúy
Body	Yoe
Bones	Oakcan
Bowels	Onúggesh
Brain	Opin
Breath	Nowwetting, or nowwettywich
Breech	Peckqueen dorsow
Breast	Wheyóe
Cheeks	Warbím
Chin	Utchwar
Eye	Wiskínky
Eye that squints	Annooch
Ear	Nóndawar

VOCABULARY.

English.	Chippeway.
Eyelid	Péwyar
Eyebrow	Gwátso
Face	Meechaw
Fundament	Meedséywort
Fingers	Argátso
Foot, or feet	Ozett
Gall	Marchéw
Hand	Armóche
Heart	Oathty
Hair	Lissy
Head	Eshtergóan
Hips	Tarbatch
Head, bald	Wematishtergóan
Knee	Puttwar
Lips	Meemoáche
Lungs	Seegwa
Leg	Ocárt
Liver	Quinch
Mouth	Meessey
Nails of fingers and toes	Narb
Neck	Shemmor

VOCABULARY.

English.	Chippeway.
Nostrils	Pecktópe
Nose	Yotch
Navel	Pinneck
Ribs	Ashíngo
Skull	Eshteroáthcan
Sinews	Atteese
Skin	Pokkikkin
Teeth	Weebitt
Thighs	Oquarme
Thumbs	Mitchea
Throat	Squissow
Toes	Tarwárchewort
Tongue	Ooton
Veins	Weebórso, or neatissum
Wrist	Annánk

VOCABULARY.

Names of Animals, &c.

English.	Chippeway.
Animal between a dog and a wolf	Wabátch
Ants, and all small insects	Mannetónce
Buck, or male deer	Ayarbéy awashkúsh
Beaver robe	Amik woygán, or amik oakónus
Bear,	Mackquáh
Bear, cub	Mackquacónce or mackónce
Beaver	Amik
Beaver skin	Appiminiquy
Beaver eater	Quickwahay
Birds, all small	Pennyshance
Buffalo	Péshshekey
Cat, wild	Peshshéw
Cat, tame	Cúshecance
Crow	Cark cark
Carp	Narmáybin
Crane	Kitchee cárbo
Duck, wild	Sheshíb
Dog	Anim

VOCABULARY.

English.	Chippeway.
Dog, puppy	Animónce
Deer	Awashkésh
Elk	Moouse
Eggs	Wark
Eagle	Meegeezes
Flesh of animals	Weass
Fur of animals	Oyan
Feathers of birds	Pequim
Fox	Assínbo
Frog	Muckkikkée
Fish	Kegónce
Fisher	Ochíck
Fowl, or birds	Pénnyshis
Fish, white	Artúkkameg
Goose, wild	Neecárk
Hog	Coocóoche
Hair of animals	Opeeway
Hide of animals	Weeyan
Hare	Wapóos
Horse	Ogashy
Loon	Maunk
Marten	Warbeshánce

VOCABULARY.

English.	Chippeway.
Mink	Shángwoitch
Musquash, or mush rat	Háwoyzask
Otter	Nekeek
Partridge	Peenay
Pickeril	Ogánce
Peltry, or robe made of fur	Woygan
Pike	Keenonjey
Plover	Guéveshew
Racoon	Asseeban
Skunk, or pole cat	Sheecark
Sturgeon	Onnemay
Snakes	Keenaypickneeshey
Skin of animals	Nink
Squirrel	Opickquoy
Swan	Kitchee meework
Tongue of animals	Sawwétch
Tail of animals	Warmeech
Turkey	Weenecobbo
Trout	Narmáyguiss
Wing of birds	Gwimbítch
Wolf	Mawhíngon

Merchandise.

English.	Chippeway.
Arm bands	Kitchee wáybesun
Axe	Ajáckquoit
Ball, or large shot	Kitchee ánwin
Brass wire	Pewarbickcónce
Beads	Mannetoo menánce
Broaches	Paunéa
Breech clout	Oncean
Blanket	Waperwóyan
Comb	Penárquan
Coat	Piskawágan
Canoe awl	Meecóose
Fire steel	Squíttycan
Finger ring	Zenzéebisson
Gun flint	Powwabickcóon
Gum	Pickkéw
Gun	Baskéyzegan

VOCABULARY.

English.	Chippeway.
Gartering	Arcoquóshergan
Gunpowder, or black dust	Mackcutty, or mackcutty pingo
Gun worms	Teakíagun
Hair plates	Saggobánwan
Hawk bells	Pewarbeneech
Horn	Pendycutty
Hats	Oweoathcoan
Kettle, or pot	Akeek
Knife, or knives	Mókoman
Knife, crooked	Wakéckuman
Lines for a net	Shenowantágan
Leggons, or stockings	Mittasse
Looking glasses	Warbermoone
Needles	Shaboonegun
Net for fishing	Assubbub
Ribbons, or silk	Sénnebar
Rum, or brandy	Scótaywábo, or Squittaywábo
Spear	Eshcan
Shot	Sheesheebanwín
Stroud blue	Mannetoo woygán

VOCABULARY.

English.	Chippeway.
Stroud, red	Míshwoygán
Shirt	Parbóckerwoyán
Tomahawk	Warcóckquoite, or Warcóckquoite Opoygan
Tobacco	Assáymer
Thread	Assúb
Vermilion	Ozonnemon
Wristbands	Annán

VOCABULARY.

Table of Words.

English.	Chippeway.
Army, or number of people assembled together	Barthtiárje
Adultery	Keemótegun
Air	Shaquoit
Ashes	Pamótay wáybegun
Arch (part of a circle)	Nondárgay
Aunt	Ergúshemin
Absent	Cáwween áppay
All	Cockinnór
Abuse, to abuse	Mecártay
All together	Cockinnór marmó
Alive	Pemártus
Ashamed, to be ashamed	Newemo
Any	Apáckcan, or han
Alike, or equal	Tabiscoach
Again, or yet	Mćenewatch
Alone, at, or only	Aighter or unter
Always, or wherever	Cargonéek, or memármo
After, or afterwards	Ningoot
And	Ashea

VOCABULARY.

English.	Chippeway.
A and The	Páyshik
Another	Ningootch
Alone, or I myself	Nin aighter
Above, or high	I'shpemeg
Also, too	Guyyea
Book, letter, paper	Marseynáygan
Bread, or flour	Pockquoísigan
Broth, or soup	Shoanárboop
Branches of a tree	Meetecónce
Brother	Shemayn
Bark of a tree	Wigwass
Bark, fire bark	Scótay wigwass
Boy	Oskenáygay
Battle	Shamishcart
Bag	Múshcomat
Barrel	Owentágun
Bridge	Warmeek
Basket, or hand bowl	Wapátch
Bed	Péshshemo
Bottle	Mótay
Bay, or road for vessels	Assénjey
Box of wood, or bark, or rum keg	Meteek múshcomat, or muccuck.
Blue	Talónjay
Bald	Parnín
Bad, or wicked	Matchee

VOCABULARY.

English.	Chippeway.
Bitter	Matooch
Bright, or light	Meeshárquoit
Barren, not bearing fruit	Matchee wáybegun
Big, or great	Menditoo
Black	Mackcútty
Blind	Warbermenéech
Broad	Hamatchey
Bottom	Haundwatchey
Busy	U'ngwoitch
Because	Mewinch
But	Moszáck
By and by	Panimár
Below	Opármey
Beyond, or far off	Awassa, or awassa woy'ta
Before	Awáshshemon
Behind	Ningôochum
Between	Icktum guichum
Besides	Metách, or menoche
Canoe	Cheeman
Country	Tunnockáy
Chief, or captain	Ojúmaw, or O'kemaw
Cup, or bark bowl	Onágun
Cloud, or grand cover	Kenárbo
Cable, or big rope	Kitchee assubbub
Copper, iron, or brass	Pewárbick
Croud	Nepewárnoondájewort

VOCABULARY.

English.	Chippeway.
Cabin, hut, or house	Wigwaum
Current of water	Sedgwin
Companion, or friend	Neejee, or Neecarnis
Courage	Haguámissey or Taguámissey
Child, or children	Queebesince
Corn, Indian	Medármin
Covetous, or greedy	Sazárgesay
Calm	Annywattin
Cunning	Matchee weebézesay
Coarse (not fine)	Matchee arpeech
Cold	Geessennar
Come here	Ondass
Can it, is it, was it	Nar
Carrying place, or portage	Onúggemeg
Devil, or Bad Spirit	Matchee Mannitoo
Daughter	Indongway, or Darniss
Dust, or powder	Pingo
Day, fine	Meeno geesshegat
Day, bad	Matchee geesshegat
Day, or days	Ogúnnegat
Day, dawn of	Thurénsera
Dart	Aysquish
Dew	Misquoitch
Debt, or trust	Marsennahatch, or Marsennáygan
Door, shut the door	Squendum
Dish	Mackcóan

VOCABULARY.

English.	Chippeway.
Down (on the ground)	Doutch
Dear, or too much	Ozóme
Done, gone, or past	Shyyár, or shárshyyar
Dark	Onárgushey
Drunk	Squibby, or Osquibby
Dressed, or ripe	Keejetty
Drowsy, (I am drowsy)	Nepárhar
Dry, or thirsty	Sparchtay
Deaf	Chartch
Dead	Nepoo
Deep	Anneycheewoatch
Edge	Gatsotes
Enemy, or bad heart	Matchee Oathty
English	Saggonash
Earth	Mattoyash
Easy	Meenwéndesay
Enough	Mee
Empty	Cawween mooshkenay
Equal, or alike	Tabiscoach
Each	Papay'jit
Flour, or bread	Pockquoísigan
Fat, oil, or grease	Pimmethy
Food	Méjimmim
Fever	Mishquoishártay
Fear, to fear, he is afraid	Keezáycus

VOCABULARY.

English.	Chippeway.
Fruit	Pinneesh
Feast	Wisseneet
Friend, or companion	Neejee, or Necárnis
Fool, he is a fool	Keepártesee
Flood of water	Chingwim
Family	Nepewoajánis
Father	Nócey
French, or builders of vessels	Waymístergoash
Fathom (a measure)	Euníck
Female, or woman	E'quoy
Fork, or prong stick	Cáwmeek meeteek
Fire	Scótay, or squitty
Flint stone	Pewarmickcoon
Fort, or tower	Wakáygon
Fond, I am fond	Nezárgea
Free, or generous	Ajáckquoy
Fine (not coarse)	Arpeech
Few	Memárjis
Fresh (not stale)	Meecheeweass
Full	Mooshquenay
Formerly, long time ago	Maywísher
Grease, fat, or oil	Pimmethy
Grapes	Minnishish
Girl	E'quoysince
God, or Great Spirit	Kitchee Mannitoo
Gold, or fine yellow metal	Kitchee jónia

VOCABULARY.

English.	Chippeway.
Great, good	Kitchee, or nishshishshín
Green	Achíb
Great, or big	Menditoo
Globe, the earth	Warbegúm
Gone, past, or done	Shyyar, or sharshyyar
Harbour	Pejárcan
Health	Pemártus
Herb, or grass	Nepísh, or mejásk
Hell, or place of bad spirits	Kitchee squíttyung
Half, or part	Arbittár
Home, or dwelling	A'shemich
Hill	Anneech
Husband, or master of weakness	Nabaim
Hole	March
Huckleberries	Shóamin
Hard, cruel; it is hard or cruel	Sánnegat
Handsome	Sasay'ga
Heavy	Pestérquan
Hot, or warm	Geeshártay
Hungry, thin, lean	Bócketty
He, him, she, or her	Ween
Here	Omár, or owáy
How, or how do you do?	Waygush, or way way
How many, or how much	Tawnimilik
Here and there	Pay payshik

VOCABULARY.

English.	Chippeway.
Have, had	Arthty
High, or above	I'shpemeg
Island	Min'nesey
Ice	Mequárme
Indians	Nishinnorbay
Journey, to go a journey	Marchián
Justice, or truth	Gwoyack
Idle, or lazy	Kíttim
Jealous	Pejármoach
I, me, or my	Nin, nee, or nee, nee
I, myself, or alone	Nin aighter
If	Késhpin
Indeed	Hapádgey
Immediately, or very soon	Weebátch
In	Pendeek
It is true, or right, or very well	Kaygait, kay, or meegwoyack
I have	Kaygo
I have not	Ka, kaygo
Is it, was it, can it	Nar
Knot of wood	Mushqucewórmeteek
King, or great chief	Gósenan
Lake	Sakíegan
Lightning, or quick fire	Squitty annacook

VOCABULARY.

English.	Chippeway.
Loss, to lose	Winnetoon
Leaves	Nepeech
Life	Noochimmoin
Love, to love	Zárgay, or zargeytoon
Land	Onjee
Lean, hungry, or thin	Bócketty
Little, small	Pongay
Light (not heavy)	Cáwween pestérquan
Light, or bright	Meeshárquoit
Lazy, or idle	Kíttim
Last	Ingwitch, or awass
Long	Keenónje
Lame	Armooch
Low	Appywick
Long since	Sharshyyar
Lately, or now	Nogóme
Lewd, or unwise	Cáwween annobóycassey
Male	Ayarbéy
Middle	Amáng
Music	Agummeweech
Merchandize	Huncúshigon, or annacótchigon
Milk, or the sap of the breast	Tootooshonárbo
Medicine	Maskikkee
Mistress, or wife	Mentimóyey
My wife, or mistress	Mentimóyamish
Mouth	Warbun

English.	Chippeway.
Moon	Geezus
Mat made of rushes	Woyzáskquish
Mother	Ningay
Man	Ninnee
Montreal (a town in Canada)	Monyny'yank
Morning	Keejay'p
Mountain	Espeo'ckay
Mud	Onjeech
Many	Márnay
Much, or a great deal	Népewar, or gwotch
Mine, belonging to me	Weechópe
Make haste	Weebittán, or ha weebittán
Me, my, or I	Nin, nee, or nee, nee.
News, or intelligence	Mergummegat
Name	Shenecazeau
Night	Debbikat
Nest, bird's nest	Wesshepátchta
Noise	Tonbingesay
Nothing, no, or not	Cáwween, or Ka
New, or strange	Nobeetch, or pockean
Narrow	Agússin
Near, or nigh	Payshéw
Not yet	Kámarchey
Now, or lately	Nogóme
Never	Cáwwickcá, or cássawickcá

VOCABULARY.

English.	Chippeway.
Oil, fat, or grease; or to be fat	Pímmethy
Old, he is old	Kcewáency
Out, or without	Accochink
Of	An
Oh! oh!	Taw! waw!
Only, at, or alone	Aighter, or unter
Our, us, or we	Neennerwind
One, the, a, or an	Páyshik
Pity, or sorrow	Cushkéndum
Part, or half	Arbittár
Pain	Daggow'wemeech
Plenty	Cúshcowait
Paint	Zawnúm
Peace	Meecho
Pipe	Opóygan
Portage, or carrying place	Onúggemeg
Peninsula	Minnesin
Poison, or the taste of the bad swelling	Matchee pattso
Paddle, or small oar	A'bboy
Priest, or Master of Life's man	Kitchee Mannitoo Ninnee
Pack, or bundle of skins	Meekintárgan
Present, or gift	Achímmey
Pledge	Assinjégo
Price, what price, how many, or how much	Andersoy

VOCABULARY.

English.	Chippeway.
Pleasure	Armeetso
People, or nation	Nondájewot
Permission	Gar
Patient	Ardátch
Proof	Chárno
Poor	Kitchee Mórgussey
Proud	Ish'pemeech
Pregnant	Mooshkey
Past, gone, done	Shyyár, or sháshyyár
Perhaps	Cánnebatch
Plural	Woke
Quiet, all is quiet	Súggermarsh
Quick	Annacook
Rock weed, or tripe de rôche	Haw'wercoon
Rice, Indian	Menómon
River	Seepee
Robe made of peltry	Woygán, or oakónus
Road	Meekan
Raft of wood	Nepewameteek
Rain	Kimmeewan
Rocks	Essíngo
Rushes	Woyzásk
Roots of trees	Watáppy
Roots, a figurative expression for the affections of the heart which entwine about each other	Waterwawadoossin

VOCABULARY.

English.	Chippeway.
Rapid, or strong current of water	Pówwetink
Ready	Guy'oxim
Rotten	Dadge
Round	Omích
Red	Misquitty, or mísquy
Rough	Guachootch
Raw, or unripe	Kakeejetty
Ripe, or dressed	Keejetty
Stone	Assín
Soup, or broth	Shoanárboop
Sense, or understanding	Annabóycassey
Sap of the breast, or milk	Tootooshomarbo
Star	Annúnk
Shame	Acheek
Stranger	Péwithay
Shade	Angwoitch
Shell	Atch
Sky	Esh'pea
Sleep	Nepán
Sugar, or sweet	Scezeebóckquoit, or seezequar
Salt	Sheotágan
Soldier, warrior, or brave man	Shemágonish
Sister	Shemay'nce
Strong, or strength	Múshkowar
Summer, or spring	Menókemeg
Stumps of trees	Mátwort

VOCABULARY.

English.	Chippeway.
Storm	Matchee geeshegar
Slay, an Indian carriage	Tarbinnáck
Spoon	Támmickquoin
Son	Jánis
Sand	Dárjey
Ship, or great canoe	Kitchee náberquoin
Shoes (Indian)	Maukissin
Sword, or great knife	Kitchee mókoman
Sea, or great unbounded lake	Kitchee gammink
Smoke, or fire fog	Keenárbittay
Sail of a ship	Kitchee náberquoin parbóckerwoyan
Snow	Going
Sun, or great light	Geessessey
Soft	Charbeech
Sad	Cushkendummermau
Sorrow, or pity	Cushkendum
Savage, or wild	Matcheewa
Small, or little	Hagúshenonce, or pongay
Sharp	Weemátch
Smooth	Narnín
Sour	Nebítch
Sudden	I'shmick
Slow	Kíttermish
Surprising	Towwácktowar
Short	Dáckquoy
Strange, or new	Nobeetch, or pockan

VOCABULARY.

English.	Chippeway.
Such	Shenárgussey
Sick	Aquoisee
She, her, he, or him	Ween
Tower or fort	Wakaygon
Truth, or justice	Gwoyack
Trade	Artawway
Trader	Artawway winnin
Thunder	Tarbishár
Tobacco pouch	Kispetawgan
Thief; he is a thief	Keemôtay
Trees, or wood	Meteek
Thoughts	Waybissay, or waybeczczay
Thing, or things	Kaygoshish
To-morrow	Warbunk
Tame	Jimmenin
Thin, hungry, or lean	Bocketty
True; to be true	Deb'woy
This, or that	Mor, or morndar
They, them, or ye	Weenewar
There, at that place	Woity, or awoity
The, a, an, or one	Páyshik
To	Ojey
Thou, or you	Keen, kee, or kee kee
Too little	Ozóme pongay
Too, or also	Guyyea
Too much	Ozóme

VOCABULARY.

English.	Chippeway.
Together	Marmo
Thank you	Meegwoitch
Urine	Mecssay
Valley	Amarcheep
Virgin	Quéwescence
Voice, or the echo of the breath	Tarpoach
Village	Narpoon
Unripe, or raw	Kakeejetty
Unwise, or lewd	Cáwween annaboycassey
Unlucky, or unfortunate	Basquecenewar
Unjust, or wrong	Cáwween gwoyack
Under	Otárpeet
Unto	Un'towarch
Upon	Ish'carmooch
Very well, or it is true, or right	Meegwoyyack, kay, or kaygait
Very soon, or immediately	Weebatch
Us, we, our, all of us	Neennerwind
Wife, or mistress	Mentimoy'ey
Water	Nippee
Wind	Noetting
Wound	Aquish
War, to go to war, to fight, or quarrel	Mecártay
Woods	Menópemeg
Wine, or blood red broth	Misquoyshoanarboop

VOCABULARY.

English.	Chippeway.
Whore, or bad woman	Matchee móyamee
Winter, or year	Bebóne
Well of water	Sagoyb
Word	Cáza
Wing	Gwimbitch
Witness, you are a witness	Ken'dersay
World, the other world	Pockcan worroc'kay, or pockcan tunnoc'kay
Wide	Packquoím
Weary, or tired	Nowwenday'shon
Wild, or savage	Matcheewa
Warm, or hot	Geeshar'tay
Wet	Neepeeweenoon
Willing, to be willing	Can'nar, or cun'ner
White	Warbishcár
Weak	Cáwween mush'kowar
Wild	Carnaboycus
We, us, or our	Neennerwind
Who, or who is that?	Way'nin
What, or what now?	Hawwaneeyaw, tar'nin, tar'neyau, or way'gonin
Where	Aúnday
When, or whence	Tan'nepy
Why	Cannatoo
Wherever, or always	Cargoneek, or memar'mo
Was it, is it, can it	Nar

VOCABULARY.

English.	Chippeway.
Young (offspring)	Wiskon'kissey
Yesterday	Pitchynar'go
Young man, or men	Doskeennerway'mug
Ye, they, or them	Weennewar
Ye, your	Kéennerwind
Yes	Angay'mer, or Nan'gaymer
Yellow	Jonia
Yet, or again	Meenewatch

English	Chippeway
To amuse, or play	Athtergain
To account	Metashwárbermy
To approve; I approve	Mornooch nezar'gay
To assist	Mawwinnewah
To alter, or change	Mishcoot
To affront	Nishcar'teyan
To answer, or attend to	Noneydone
To ask, I ask	Nindooton, or nindootimond
To ascend	Negádeja
To abandon, or forsake	Pack'itan
To arrive at a place	Takooshin
To arrive by land	Keekeepejar'can
To arrive by water	Sharshyyar' new'ebens
To avoid	Yaquoy
To attack	Jimmim
To be vexed; I am vexed	Nischeárteseyyan

VOCABULARY.

English.	Chippeway.
To believe	Indenéndum gwoyack
To bawl	Tonbíngus
To be told	Ecárto
To begin	Ethetum war'march
To bend	Marchím
To be willing	Can'nar, or cun'ner
To betray all	Matchee arpeech chickwar'woke
To beat, or bruise	Packettywaun
To bring, or fetch	Nartín, or Petoon
To bind, or tie	Tackan'nin
To break, or tear	Bowwískar
To bite	Quoyjím
To build	Gowwcájetoon
To barter	Gudgymárdat
To boil	Zepeeooch
To borrow	Carmatch'ey
To burn	Squitty árbach
To beg (you beg)	Keenandóton
To bathe	Nepewoy'awat
To be unconcerned, or indifferent about a thing	Mornooch towwárch
To cut	Kiskejune
To call	Nandootum
To choose	Tucku'nnin
To cure	Zársquoy

English.	Chippeway.
To catch	Kecásquin
To clean	Warbermeech
To chew	Wis'semeg
To come on	Ondash'in
To carry	Keemárjemet
To close	Dusquin
To converse	Debárchim, or debárchemon
To conquer	Ninnowátchim
To dance	Neméh
To drown	Nepewooch
To divide	Arbitórch
To dig	Achím
To dwell, or stay	Appay
To defend	Mushkáwesay
To dream	Charmeech
To drop	Char'quoy
To depart	Gamar'char
To drink	Mínniquah
To dip	Marchtooch
To elect	Keetárpeech
To embark	Boossin
To experience	Candan
To expect	Indenéndumsee
To eat	Wíssinnin

VOCABULARY.

English.	Chippeway.
To freeze	Mushcow'wartin
To find	Warbennecó
To fast	Bockettyneech
To fish	Bockettywaun
To feel	Tarpín, or peach
To fall	Pónkissin
To float	Arnooch
To follow	Weegewach'in
To forget; I forgot	Newinnemeecoossay
To foretell; I foretell	Newárbemoach
To fetch, or bring	Nartín, or petoon
To fly	Zeewítch
To grow	Ameechet
To grind	Ojít
To give	Dármissey
To go, I will go	Es'zar, or Gúddeszar
To go by water	Pamískian, or pemískar
To go by land	Papamótay
To get up, or rise	Goníshcar
To govern	Tibárimaw
To hide	Cannawéndan
To hold	Jingwim
To hate	Neshárquish
To hear	Stootewar, or nondágaitch
To hurt	Naw'wameetch

VOCABULARY.

English.	Chippeway.
To hang	Peechúganub
To hunt	Géosay
To hit	Mátwoit
To have	Arwayyor
To interpret	Kitchee ungwoitch undárjewort
To jump	Abooch
To join, I join	Neewo
To keep	Gannewaínnemar
To kill	Gúnnesar
To know, you know	Keecannawéndan
To kick	Achíp
To lend	Mishcow'womeech
To love; love	Zárgay, or zárgeytoon
To long to see, or wish	Badásh
To lose; loss	Wínnetoon
To lift	Es'termeech
To learn	E'shpermeech
To lead	Acheech
To lie down	Neparhan
To lie, a falsity	Cáwween deb'woy
To laugh	Pawpy'
To meet	Neewatch
To make fire and cook	Pooterway chebóckwoy

VOCABULARY.

English.	Chippeway.
To make, or do	Ojeytoon, or tojeytoon
To measure	Apín
To melt	Acheemeech
To mend	Packquoy mowachin
To mix	Packquoítso
To marry	Tuckunnu'mkewish
To make water	Meesesay
To neglect	Winnemawatch
To own	Guddypen'dan, or dépendan
To open	Pameech, or hapitch
To place, or put	Acktone, or neech
To pull	Ajárme
To pay	Guddypa'rhan
To please	Mirrowerrindan
To push	Meetso
To pass	Pisquitch
To pierce	Chagworm
To pinch	Chímmeney
To promise	Nebebeewoy
To perspire	Matootoo
To return	Tercus'henan, or guabeecheway
To raise	Ishpin
To receive	Ajímmoach

VOCABULARY.

English.	Chippeway.
To row	Pemíshkar
To rejoice	Papyan
To run	Squamích
To read	Daguoítso
To revolt	Etummecártey
To ride	Annyscoop
To release	Pejárkemet
To rise or get up	Gónishear
To repudiate, to throw away	Waybenán
To shake	Písquemeetch
To stand up	Pásserquoin
To sail	Pemíshearmooch
To spit	Warmar'ch
To seek	Warchar'ch
To stand	Andátch
To seize	Ajímmenin
To stab	Batchcypehone
To split	Chippauk
To shew	Serpárgusscy
To shut	Cupperharne
To sing	Nájemoon
To sink	Nondágat
To satisfy	Neminwaíndesee
To sit down, or sit you down	Mantetáppy
To send	Marchetoon
To smoke a pipe	Suggersoy

VOCABULARY.

English.	Chippeway.
To swim	Squabeech
To see	Wabemát, or wabemór
To speak	Debárchim, or debárchemon
To smell	Iaquítch
To say; what did you say? when spoke angrily	Ickeetóyan
To stink; you stink, or your sentiments are offensive	Keeméchawich
To strike	Keebárcham
To steal	Keemótyan
To sleep	Nepán
To tie, or bind	Tackannin
To touch	Chewwar
To tell	Gudjey
To think	In'denind, or indenéndum
To throw away; to repudiate	Waybenán
To take	Tarpenán
To understand	Ncesstootewar
To view, or examine well my mind	Wabindán
To vex	Annascar'tissey, or níshcar'tissey
To win	Warmatt
To watch	Warbennís, or warbennét
To wash	Zaquébenan

English.	Chippeway.
To work	Tojcytoon, or gúsketoon
To want	Guy'yossey
To weep	Marrny'
To walk, or go	Pamósay
To weigh	Quois'ciquen
To wish, or long to see	Badásh

VOCABULARY.

Table of Words.

Chippeway.	English.
Abboy	Paddle, or small oar
Ajack'quoit	Axe
Annaboy'casscy	Sense, or understanding
Aník	Arm
Appimíniquy	Beaver skin
Ayarbéy awashkésh	Buck, or male deer
Amík	Beaver
Assénjey	Bay, (harbour for canoes)
Aním	Dog
Animónce	Dog, puppy
Aysquish	Dart
Awashkésh	Deer
Annooch	Eye that squints
Argátso	Fingers
Assínbo	Fox
Artik'kameg	White fish
Arcoquosh'ergan	Gartering
Armoche	Hand
Arbittár	Half, or part
Anneech	Hill
A'shemich	Home, or dwelling
Akeek	Kettle, or pot

VOCABULARY.

Chippeway.	English.
Ayarbéy	Male
Annacótchigon, or huncúshigon	Merchandise
Amáng	Middle
Agúmmeweech	Music
Assúbúb	Net for fishing
Assúb	Thread
Achimmey	Present, or gift
Assinjégo	Pledge
An'dersoy, or tawnymilik	Price; what price? how many? how much
Armeetso	Pleasure
Ashin'go	Ribs
Asseeban	Racoon
Amík woygán, or amik oakónus	Beaver robe
Aquísh	Wound
Attees	Sinews
Annúnk	Star
Assín	Stone
Acheek	Shame
Angwoitch	Shade
Atch	Shell
Artawway	Trade
Artawway winnin	Trader
Assay'mer	Tobacco
Amarcheep	Valley
Annánk	Wrist
Annán	Wristbands

VOCABULARY.

Chippeway.	English.
Annywattin	Calm
Anneycheewoatch	Deep
Achíb	Green
Armooch	Lame
Ajack'quoy	Free, or generous
Appywick	Low
Agússin	Narrow
Ardátch	Patient
Arpeech	Fine, not coarse
Annacook	Quick
Ae'quoisee	Sick
Apackhan, or han	Any
Awoíty, or woíty	There; at a place
Aighter, or unter	Only, at, alone
Aúnday	Where
Angáymer, or nángaymer	Yes
Awashemon	Before
An	Of
Awa'ss, or ingwitch	Last
Awa'ssa, or awa'ssa woy'ta	Beyond, or far off
Accochink	Out, or without
Arthty	Have, had
Ashea	And
Athtergain	To amuse, or play
Arbitórch	To divide
Arwayyor	To have
Achím	To dig
An'yscoop	To ride

VOCABULARY.

Chippeway.	English.
Appay	To dwell, or stay
Amooch	To float
Acheech	To lead
Amecchet	To grow
Achíp	To kick
Abooch	To jump
Apín	To measure
Ajárme	To pull
Ajímmoach	To receive
Ajímmenin	To seize
Andátch	To stand
Ac'ktone, or neech	To place, or put
Annascar'tissey, or níshcártissey	To vex
Acheemeech	To melt
Báskey'zegan	Gun
Bebo'ne	Winter, or year
Barthtiar'je	Army, or number of people assembled together
Bócketty	Hungry, thin, lean
Basqueenewar	Unlucky, or unfortunate
Bowwis'kar	To break, or tear
Bóckettyneech	To fast
Batcheypehone	To stab
Badásh	To long to see, or wish
Bóckettywaun	To fish
Boossin	To embark

VOCABULARY.

Chippeway.	English.
Cushkéndum	Sorrow, or pity
Cheeman	Canoe
Cúshecance	Tame cat
Cark cark	Crow
Chingwím	Flood of water
Cáwmeck metcek	Fork, or prong stick
Coocooshe	Hog
Cúshcowait	Plenty
Cáwween, or ka	Nothing, no, not
Cáza	Word
Cáwween áppay	Absent
Cockinnór	All
Cockinnór marmó	All together
Chartch	Deaf
Cáwween mooshkenay	Empty
Cáwween pestérquan	Light (not heavy)
Cáwween annaboy'cassey	Lewd, or unwise
Charbeech	Soft
Cushkendúmmerman	Sad
Cáwween gwoyack	Unjust, or wrong
Cáwween mush'kowar	Weak
Carnayboy'cus	Wild
Cargoneek, or memármo	Always, wherever
Cáwwická, or cássawickcá	Never
Cannatoo	Why
Can'nebatch	Perhaps
Chárno	Proof

VOCABULARY.

Chippeway.	English.
Can'ner, or cun'ner	Willing, to be willing
Candan	To experience
Charmeech	To dream
Char'quoy	To drop
Cannawéndan	To hide
Cáwween deb'woy	To lie (a falsity)
Chagworm	To pierce
Chímmeney	To pinch
Chíppauk	To split
Cupperharne	To shut
Chewwar	To touch
Carmátchey	To borrow
Deb'bikat	Night
Doskeennerway'mug	Young man, or men
Daggow'wemeech	Pain
Dar'jey	Sand
Dar'niss, or indong'way	Daughter
Dadge	Rotten
Dáckquoy	Short
Doutch	Down, on the ground
Deb'woy	True, to be true
Dus'quin	To close
Debar'chim, or debar'chemon	To converse
Daguoit'so	To read
Depen'dan, or gú.ldypendan	To own
Dar'missey	To give

VOCABULARY.

Chippeway.	English.
Euníck	Fathom (a measure)
Ergush'shemin	Aunt
E'quoy	Woman, or female
E'quoysince	Girl
Eshtergóan	Head
Espeoc'kay	Mountain
Essíngo	Rocks
Eshteroath'can	Skull
E'shcan	Spears
Esh'pea	Sky
Es'zar, or gúddeszar	To go; I will go
Ethetum war'march	To begin
Es'termeech	To lift
Esh'permeech	To learn
Etummecar'tey	To revolt
Ecar'to	To be told
Gósenan	King, or great chief
Gwat'so	Eyebrow
Gatsoates	Edge
Gwoyack	Justice, or truth
Geezus	Moon
Guéveshew	Plover
Going	Snow
Geessesscy	Sun, or great light
Gwimbítch	Wing, of birds
Geessennar	Cold

VOCABULARY.

Chippeway.	English.
Geeshar'tay	Hot, or warm; to make hot or warm
Guy'oxim	Ready
Guachootch	Rough
Gar	Permission
Guyyea	Also, too
Gwotch, or népewar	Much, or a great deal
Gudggymárdat	To barter
Guabeechcway, or tercúshenan	To return
Gowweájetoon	To build
Gamar'char	To depart
Guy'yossey	To want
Géosay	To hunt
Gannewain'nemar	To keep
Gun'nesar	To kill
Guddypar'han	To pay
Guddypen'dan, or dépendan	To own
Gudjey	To tell
Gonish'kar	To rise, or get up
Gúsketoon, or tójeytoon	To work
Gúddeszar, or Es'zar	To go, I will go
Huncush'igon, or annacotch'igon	Merchandise
Hagua'missey, or táguámissey	Courage
Háwoyzask	Musquash, or musk rat
Haw'wercoon	Tripe de rôche, or rock weed
Hamátchey	Broad

VOCABULARY.

Chippeway.	English.
Haundwátchey	Bottom
Hagúshenonce	Small
Hawwaneeyaw, tarnin, tarneyau, or way'gonin	What, or what now?
Han, or apackcan	Any
Hapadjey	Indeed
Hapitch, or pameech	To open
Ha weebittan, or weebittan	Make haste
Indong'way, or dar'niss	Daughter
Jánis	Son
Jónia	Yellow
Ish'pemeg	High, or above
Ingwítch, or awáss	Last
Ish'pemeech	Proud
I'shmick	Sudden
Jimmenin	Tame
Is'quamach	Belly
Icktum guichum	Between
I'shearmooch	Upon
In'denind, or indenen'dum	To think
Indenen'dumsee	To expect
Jímmim	To attack
Jingwím	To hold
Ishpin	To raise
Jaquítch	To smell
Indenen'dum gwoyack	To believe a thing true

VOCABULARY.

Chippeway.	English.
Ickkeetoyan	To say; what did you say? when spoken angrily
Kes'coneek	Broken arm
Keemótegun	Adultery
Kitchee anwin	Ball, or large shot
Kitchee carbo	Crane (a bird)
Keenar'bo	Cloud, or grand cover
Kitchee assubbub	Cable, or big rope
Keegónce	Fish
Keepartesee	Fool; he is a fool
Kitchee mannitoo	God, or Great Spirit
Kitchee jónia	Gold, or fine yellow metal
Kitchee squittyung	Hell, or place of bad spirits
Keejayp	Morning
Keenonjey	Pike, a fish
Kitchee mannitoo ninnee	Priest, or Master of Life's man
Kimmeewan	Rain
Keenaypick'neeshey	Snakes
Kitchee meework	Swan
Kitchee mókoman	Sword, or great knife
Kitchee gammink	Sea, or great unbounded lake
Keenárbittay	Smoke, or fire fog
Kitchee náberquoin parbock'er-woyan	Sail of a ship
Kitchee náberquoin	Ship, or great canoe
Keemôtay	Thief; he is a thief

VOCABULARY. 263

Chippeway.	English.
Kispetaw'gan	Tobacco pouch
Keezay'cus	Fear; to fear; he is afraid
Ken'dersay	Witness; you are a witness
Kitchee, or nishshishshin	Great, or good
Kitchee way'besun	Armbands
Kittim	Idle, or lazy
Keenónge	Long
Keewácncy	Old, he is old
Kitchee mor'gussey	Poor
Kakeejetty	Raw, or unripe
Keejetty	Ripe, or dressed
Kíttermish	Slow
Keen, kee, or kee kee	Thou, or you
Ka, or ca'wween	No, not; nothing
Késhpin	If
Kaygoshish	Thing, or things
Kaygait, kay, or meegwoyack	It is true, or truly
Kamar'chey	Not yet
Keennerwind	Ye, your
Kaygo	I have
Kakaygo	I have not
Keenandóton	To beg; you beg
Keeas'quin	To catch
Keekeepejar'can	To arrive by land
Kískejune	To cut
Keemar'jemet	To carry
Keetar'peech	To elect

Chippeway.	English.
Kitchee ungwoitch, undar'jewort	To interpret
Keemótyan	To steal
Keemeechawich	To stink; you stink, or your sentiments are offensive
Keebar'cham	To strike
Keecannawen'dan	To know; you know
Lissy	Human hair
Mejásk, or nepísh	Herb, or grass
Marchián	Journey; to go a journey
Mushqueewor'meteck	Knot of wood
Mannetónce	Ants, and all small insects
Misquy'	Blood
Mannetoo menan'ce	Beads
Mackquáh	Bear
Mackquacon'ce, or mackon'ce	Cub bear
Meetecónse	Branches of a tree
Marseynay'gan	Book, letter, or paper
Meteek múshcomat, or muccuck	Box of wood, or bark, or rum keg
Môtay	Bottle
Múshcomat	Bag
Meecoose	Canoe awls
Medar'min	Indian corn
Menómon	Indian rice
Matchee Mannitoo	Devil, or bad spirit
Misquoitch	Dew

VOCABULARY.

Chippeway.	English.
Mackcóan	Dish
Meekintar'gan	Pack, or bundle of skins
Marsennahatch or, marsennay'gan	Debt, or trust
Meeno geesshegat	Fine day
Matchee geeshegat	Bad day
Moouse	Elk
Meegeezes	Eagle
Matchee oathty	Enemy, or bad heart
Mattoyash	Earth
Meechaw	Face
Meedséywort	Fundament
Muckkikee	Frog
Mejimmim	Food
Mishquoishártay	Fever
Marchew'	Gall
Min'nishish	Grapes
March	Hole
Min'nesey	Island
Min'nesin	Peninsula
Meequorm	Ice
Mókoman	Knife, or knives
Meemoche	Lips
Mittasse	Leggons, or stockings
Maunk	Loon, (a bird)
Maskikkee	Medicine
Mentimoy'ey	Wife, or mistress
Mentimoy'amish	My wife, or mistress

VOCABULARY.

Chippeway.	English.
Meesey	Mouth
Mergummegat	News
Mackcutty, or mackcutty pingo	Gunpowder, or black dust
Meecho	Peace
Matchee pattso	Poison, or the taste of the bad swelling
Meekan	Road
Mannetoo woygan'	Blue stroud
Mishwoygan'	Red stroud
Menókemeg	Summer, or spring
Mat'wort	Stumps of trees
Mùshkowar	Strength, or strong
Matchee geesshegar	Storm
Monyny'yank	Montreal, a town in Canada
Maukissin	Indian shoes
Metcek	Trees, or wood
Mitchea	Thumbs
Meessay	Urine
Mawhin'gon	Wolf
Mecar'tay	War; to go to war; to fight, or quarrel
Menópemeg	Woods
Misquoyshoanar'boop	Wine, or blood red broth
Matchee móyamee	Whore, or bad woman
Matchee	Bad, or wicked
Matooch	Bitter
Matchee way'begun	Barren, or not bearing fruit

Chippeway.	English.
Menditoo	Big, or great
Matchee arpeech	Coarse, not fine
Matchee weebeezesay	Cunning
Meenwen'desay	Easy
Mee	Enough
Meermárjis	Few
Meecheweass	Fresh, not stale
Mooshquenay	Full
Mackcutty	Black
Meeshar'quoit	Light, or bright
Marnay	Many
Mooshkey	Pregnant
Misquy, or misquitty	Red
Matcheewa	Savage, or wild
Marmo	Together
Maunder, or mor	This, or that
Metách, or menoch	Besides
Mewinch	Because
Meenewatch	Again, or yet
Memar'mo, or cargoneek	Always, wherever
Maywísher	Long time ago, formerly, or is it long since?
Moszack	But
Meegwoyack, kay, or kaygait	It is true, or right, or very well
Meewgotch	Thank you
Mishcoot	To alter, or change
Marchetoop	To send

Chippeway.	English.
Mantetappy	To sit down, or sit you down
Meetso	To push
Mirrowerrindan	To please
Metashwar'bermy	To account
Mornooch nezar'gay	To approve; I approve
Mawwinnewah	To assist
Marchím	To bend
Matchee arpeech chickwar	To betray
Matchee arpeech chickwar'woke	To betray a number of people
Marmy'	To weep
Mornooch towwárch	To be unconcerned, or indifferent about a thing
Mushkáwesay	To defend
Mat'woit	To hit
Min'niquah	To drink
Mishcow'womeech	To lend
Marchtooch	To dip
Mushcow'wartin	To freeze
Matootoo	To perspire
Nondar'gay	Arch, part of a circle
Nowettywich, or nowwetting	Breath
Narmay'bin	Carp, a fish
Nepewarnoondájewort	Crowd
Non'dawar	Ear
Neejee, or neecarnis	Friend, or companion
Nepewoajánis	Family
Nócey	Father

VOCABULARY.

Chippeway.	English.
Nepísh, or mejásk	Herb, or grass
Nabaim'	Husband, or master of weakness
Nishinnorbay	Indians
Noochimmoin	Life
Nin'gay	Mother
Ninnee	Man
Narb	Nails of fingers and toes
Neecárk	Wild goose
Nepeech	Leaves
Nekeek	Otter
Neatissum, or weebor'so	Veins of the body
Nondájewot	People, or nation
Nepewámeteek	Raft of wood
Nink	Skin of animals
Nepan'	Sleep
Narmay'guiss	Trout
Narpoon	Village
Nippee	Water
Noetting	Wind
Newemo	Ashamed; to be ashamed
Ningootch	Another
Nezar'gea	Fond, I am fond
Nepewár, or gwotch	Much, or a great deal
Nishshishshin', or kitchee	Good, or great
Nobeetch, or pockcan	New, or strange
Narnín	Smooth
Nebítch	Sour

VOCABULARY.

Chippeway.	English.
Nepeeweenoon	Wet
Nowwenday'shon	Weary, or tired
Neepoo	Dead
Nepárhar	Drowsy; I am drowsy
Nin, nee, or nee nee	I, me, my
Nin aighter	I myself, or alone
Neennerwind	We, us, or our; all of us
Nangay'mer, or angay'mer	Yes
Nogom	Now, or lately
Ningoot	Afterwards, or after
Ningoochum	Behind
Ningootch	Another
Nar	Is it, was it, can it
Nishcar'teyan	To affront
Neeshar'quish	To hate
Nishcarteseyan	To be vexed; I am vexed
Nishcartissay, or annascartissey	To vex
Nóneydone	To answer, or attend to
Nindooton, or nindootimond	To ask; I ask
Negádeja	To ascend
Nepewoy'awat	To bathe
Neesstootewar	To understand
Ninnowatchim	To conquer
Neméh	To dance
Nepewooch	To drown
Nartín, or petoon	To fetch, or bring
Naw'wamceteh	To hurt

VOCABULARY.

Chippeway.	English.
Neewo	To join
Neparhan	To lie down
Newinnemecoossay	To forget; I forget
Newárbemoach	To foretell; I foretell
Nondágaitch, or stootewar	To hear
Neewatch	To meet
Neech, or acktone	To put, or place
Nebebeewoy	To promise
Nájemoon	To sing
Nondágat	To sink
Neminwain'desee	To satisfy
Nepa'n	To sleep
Nandootum	To call
Onágun	Bark bowl, or cup
Oakónus, or amik woygan'	Beaver robe
Opeewyesky	Beard
Onick'quick	Back
Oakcan	Bones
Opin	Brain
Oneean	Breech clout
Oskenay'gay	Boy
Owentágun	Barrel
Ojémaw, or O'kemaw	Chief
Ogunnegat	Day, or days
Ozett	Foot, or feet
Oyan	Fur of animals

VOCABULARY.

Chippeway.	English.
Ochick'	Fisher, an animal
Onuggesh	Bowels
Oathty	Heart
Opeeway	Hair of animals
Oweoathcoan	Hats
Onúggemeg	Portage, or carrying place
Ogashy	Horse
Ocárt	Leg
Onjee	Land
Onjeech	Mud
Opoy'gan	Pipe
Ogánce	Pickerill, a fish
Onnemay	Sturgeon, a fish
Opickquoy	Squirrel
Oquarme	Thighs
Outon	Tongue
Ozonnemon	Vermillion
Ozóme	Too much, or dear
Ozóme pongay	Too little
Onar'gushey	Dark
Omích	Round
Opar'mey	Below
Omár, or owáy	Here
Otárpeet	Under
Ojey	To
Ondass	Come here
Osquibby, or squibby	Drunk

VOCABULARY.

Chippeway.	English.
Ojit	To grind
Ojeytoon, or ogúbbetoon	To make, or do
Ondashin'	To come on
Pennyshance	All small birds
Pamótay way'begun	Ashes
Peckqueen dorsow	Breech
Pewarbickcónce	Brass wire
Paunéa	Broaches
Peshshekcy	Buffalo
Pesh'shemo	Bed
Penar'quan	Combs
Piskawágan	Coats
Peshshew	Wood cat
Pewar'bick	Copper, iron, or brass
Pingo	Dust, or powder
Pewyar	Eyelid
Pennyshis	Fowl, or birds
Pockquoísigan	Flour, or bread
Pinneesh	Fruit
Pequim	Feathers of birds
Pewarmickcoon	Flint stone
Powwabickcoon	Gun flints
Pickkew	Gum
Powwetink	Rapid or strong current of water
Péwithay	Stranger
Pewarbeneech	Hawk bells

VOCABULARY.

Chippeway.	English.
Peja'rcan	Harbour
Pemartus	Health
Pendycutty	Horn
Puttwar	Knee
Pecktópe	Nostrills
Pinneck	Navel
Pimmethy	Oil, fat, or grease; or to be fat
Peenay	Partridge
Pockkikkin	Skin (human)
Parbock'erwoyan'	Shirts
Pockcan worrockay, or pockcan tunnockay	The other world, or country
Pitchynar'go	Yesterday
Pester'quan	Heavy
Parmín	Bald
Pejar'moach	Jealous
Pongay, or hagush'enonce	Little, small
Páyshik	One, the, a, or an
Pockcan, or nobeetch	Strange, or new
Packquoim	Wide
Payshéw	Near, or nigh
Papay'jit	Each
Panímár	By and by
Pendeck	In
Pay, páyshik	Here, and there
Pack'itan	To abandon, or forsake
Peach, or tarpín	To feel

VOCABULARY.

Chippeway.	English.
Pon'kissin	To fall
Pamískian, or pemískar	To go by water
Papamôtay	To go by land
Peechúganub	To hang
Packettywaun	To beat
Pawpy'	To laugh
Packquoy mowachin	To mend
Packquoítso	To mix
Petóon, or nartín	To fetch, or bring
Pameech, or hapítch	To open
Pisquitch	To pass
Pemíshkar	To row
Papyan	To rejoice
Pejar'kemet	To release
Pas'serquoin	To stand up
Pemíshcarmooch	To sail
Pis quemeetch	To shake
Pamósay	To walk
Pooterway chebock'woy	To make a fire and cook
Quickwahay	Beaver eater
Queebesince	Child, or children
Quinch	Liver
Quéwescence	Virgin
Quoyjím	To bite
Quoiś ciquen	To weigh

VOCABULARY.

Chippeway.	English.
Shaquoit	Air
Shemayn	Brother
Shoanar'boop	Broth, or soup
Shemay'nce	Sister
Shamíshcart	Battle
Sedgwin	Current of water
Squendum	Door; shut the door
Sheshíb	Wild duck
Saggonash	English
Squittycan	Fire steels
Squitty, or scotay	Fire
Scotay wigwass	Fire bark
Saggoban'wan	Hair plates
Shóamin	Huckleberries
Seegwa	Lungs
Squitty annacook	Lightning, or quick fire
Sakíegan	Lake
Shenowantágan	Lines for a net
Shan'gwoitch	Mink
Shem'mor	Neck
Shaboonegun	Needles
Shenecázeau	Name
Sen'nebar	Ribbands, or silk
Scótaywa'bo, or squittywa'bo	Rum, or brandy
Seepec	River
Shecsheebanwín	Shot
Sheecark	Skunk, or pole-cat

VOCABULARY.

Chippeway.	English.
Seezeebockquoit, or seezequar	Sugar, or sweet
Sagoyb	Well of water
Sheotágan	Salt
Shemágonish	Soldier, warrior, or brave man
Squissow	Throat
Sawwétch	Tongue of animals
Sazárgesay	Greedy, or covetous
Sannegat	Hard, cruel; it is hard, or cruel
Sasay'ga	Handsome
Shenargusscy	Such
Sug'germarsh	Quiet; all is quiet
Shyyár, or shar'shyyár	Past, or gone, or done
Squibby, or Osquibby	Drunk
Sparchtay	Thirsty, or dry
Sharshyar' newebens	To arrive by water
Squittyar'bach	To burn
Sug'gersoy	To smoke a pipe
Squabeech	To swim
Serpar'gussey	To shew
Stootewar, or nondágaitch	To hear
Squamích	To run
Sharshyyár	Long since
Taguámissey, or haguámissey	Courage
Tonbin'gesay	Noise
Tunnoc'kay	Country
Teakíagun	Gun worms

VOCABULARY.

Chippeway.	English.
Tarbátch	Hips
Tootooshonarbo	Milk, or sap of the breast
Tam'mikquoin	Spoon
Tarbinnáck	Indian slay
Tarbishár	Thunder
Talon'jay	Blue
Tarwar'chewort	Toes
Thurensera	Dawn of day
Tarpoach	Voice, or the echo of the breath
Tabiscoach	Equal, or alike
Towwacktowar	Surprising
Tannepy	When, or whence
Tar'nin, tar'neyau, way'gonin, or hawwaneeyaw	What, or what now?
Tawnimilik, or andersoy	How many, what price, how much?
Taw! waw!	Oh! oh!
Tarpenán	To take
Takooshin	To arrive at a place
Tackannin	To bind, or tie
Tuckunnin	To choose
Tibárimaw	To govern
Tuckunnum'kewish	To marry
Tonbin'gus	To bawl
Tercush'enan, or guabeecheway	To return
Turpin, or peach	To feel
Tójeytoon, or gúsketoon	To work
Utchwar	Chin

VOCABULARY.

Chippeway.	English.
Un'gwoitch	Busy
Unter, or aighter	Only, at, or alone
Untowarch	Unto
Way'bissay, or waybeezesay	Thoughts
Warbunk	To-morrow
Warwích	Ankle
Warcockquoit, or warcockquoit opoygan	Tomahawk
Wabatch	An animal between a dog and a wolf
Wheeyóe	Breast
Waperwoyan'	Blankets
Wapátch	Basket, or hand bowl
Warmeek	Bridge
Wigwass	Bark of a tree
Warbim'	Cheeks
Wiskin'ky	Eyes
Wark	Eggs
Warbegum'	Globe, the earth
Weass	Flesh of animals
Wisseneet	Feast
Waymístergoash	French, or builders of vessels
Wakay'gon	Fort, or tower
Wematishtergóan	Bald head
Woygán, or oakónus	Robe made of peltry
Wapoos'	Hare

Chippeway.	English.
Weeyan	Hide of animals
Wigwaum	House, cabin, or hut
Wakeck'uman	Crooked knife
Warbermoon	Looking glasses
Winnetoon	Loss
Warbun'	Month
Woyzáskquish	Rush mat
Warbeshan'ce	Marten, an animal
Wesshepátchta	Bird's nest
Woyzásk	Rushes
Watappy	Roots of trees
Warmeech	Tail of animals
Weenecobbo	Turkey
Weebitt	Teeth
Weebor'so, or neatissum	Veins
Wiscon'kissey	Young, offspring
Warbermeneech	Blind
Weematch	Sharp
Warbishcár	White
Waterwawadoossin	Roots; a figurative expression for the affections of the heart, which entwine about each other
Ween	He, him, she or her
Weennewar	Ye, they, or them
Way'nin	Who, or who is that?
Way'gonin, hawwaneeyaw ——— tar'nin ——— Tar'neyau	What, or what now?

VOCABULARY.

Chippeway.	English.
Waygush, or way way	How, or how do you do?
Woity, or awoity	There, at that place
Weebátch	Immediately, or very soon
Weechópe	Mine, belonging to me
Woke	Plural number
Weebittan', or ha, weebittan'	Make haste
Warbermeech	To clean
Wíssemeg	To chew
Wissinnin	To eat
Weegewach'in	To follow
Warbermecó	To find
Wínnemawatch	To neglect
Warmarch	To spit
Wabindán	To view, or examine well my mind
Wabemát, or wabemór	To see
Warcharch	To seek
Warmatt	To win
Warbennís, or warbennét	To watch
Waybenán	To throw away, to repudiate
Yoe	Body
Yotch	Nose
Yaquoy	To avoid
Zenzeebisson	Finger rings
Zárgay, or zargéytoon	Love; to love

VOCABULARY.

Chippeway.	English.
Zawnum'	Paint; to paint
Zeepeeooch	To boil
Zar'squoy	To cure
Zcewitc'h	To fly
Zayquébenan	To wash

FAMILIAR PHRASES

IN THE

ENGLISH AND CHIPPEWAY LANGUAGES.

FAMILIAR PHRASES IN THE ENGLISH

English.

How do you do, friend?
In good health, I thank you.
What news?
I have none.
Have you had a good hunt this winter?
Yes, a very good hunt.
What lake did you hunt at last winter?
At the Skunk Lake.
What is there at that lake?
Beaver, but not much.
How long were you there?
Only one month.
They say there are no fish in that lake;
That is hard.
There has been a great deal of snow lately;
We have all found it hard this winter.
Did you see any strange Indians on the way?
Yes, I met five going to Lake Sturgeon.
Had they any thing with them?
No, I did not see any thing but slays.
I long to see spring, that we may go a fishing.
What lake will you fish at?
The Red Lake.

VOCABULARY.

AND CHIPPEWAY LANGUAGES.

Chippeway.

Way, way, nee neejee?
Meegwotch nóbum pemártus.
Ta'rnin mergúmmegat,?
Caw'ween a'rwayyor.
Níshshishshín géosay nógome bebóne?
Anga'ymer, O, níshshishshín.
Hawwaneeyaw sakíegan kee géosay awa'ss bebóne?
Sheecark Sakíegan.
Way'gonin woíty ha sakíegan?
Amík, cawween gwotch.
Maywísher kee appay?
Páyshik geezus aíghter.
Eca'rto ca'wween ka'ygo keegónce woity sakíegan;
Sannegat.
Nepewár going nogóme ;
Cockinnór marmó ojey candan sannegat nogóme bebóne.
Póckcan níshinnorbay kee warbema't nar?
Anga'ymer, na'rnan nee warbemór onnemay sakíegan ojey eszar.
Ka'ygoshish arthty wéenewar nar?
Ca'wween, nin ojey warberma't a'rwayyor tarbinna'ck.
Ba'dash menókemeg bóckettywaun neennerwind.
Ta'rneyau sakíegan keen bóckettywaun?
Misquíttyyang sakíegan.

VOCABULARY.

English.

Our canoes are broken;
We must make new in the spring.
There is great quantity of birch bark at the Red Lake;
Yes, but the trees are small.
How many fathom long will you make your canoe?
Perhaps three fathom.
There are many rapids at the Red Lake;
Are they hard rapids?
Here and there.
How long are you going up them?
Fifteen days.
That is long.
Bring me some tobacco;
Here is some for you.
This is English;
Yes, it is.
Sit down.
I want to smoke a pipe.
I am tired.
I will lie down.
I will get up.
I want to eat.
I want to drink.
We will make fire and cook our kettle;
It is ready;
Let us eat;
It is very good.

VOCABULARY.

Chippeway.

Cóckinnor neennerwind, O, chema'n ojey bowwískar;
Póckcan in gar ojeytoon menókemeg.
Nepewár wigwass woity Misquíttyyang Sakíegan;
Anga'ymer, hagúshenonce meteek.
Ta'wnimilík euníck kee ojeytóon chema'n?
Ca'nnebatch neesswoy euník.
Nepewár powwetink Misquíttyyang Sakíegan;
Sannegat nar powwetink?
Pay, pa'yshik.
Maywísher nar shy'yar cockinnór
Metósswoy ogúnnegat asshea na'rnan.
Débwoy maywísher.
Assa'ymer petoon;
Oway.
Maúnder Sa'ggonash;
Anga'ymer débwoy.
Manteta'ppy.
Nee, wee, súggersoy.
Nowwenda'yshon nin.
Nepa'rhan, nin.
Goyey nin goníshcar.
Nee, nee, wissínnin.
Nee, nee, mínniquah.
Pooterway chebóckwoy neennerwind;
Shashy'yar keejetty;
Haw wíssinnin;
Húnjeyta O, níshshishshin.

English.

I will go.
Are you going, friend?
Yes, but I shall return soon.
Have you any good guns?
Yes.
Let us see them?
This is broke.
Here is another;
This, I think, is a good one.
I want a paddle;
Here is one for you.
Thank you, friend.
Where is your wife?
She is dead.
Is it long since?
Last winter.
Have you any children alive?
Only one boy.
Can he hunt?
Not yet.
Where is your brother?
I saw him last winter at the Skunk's Lake;
He was killed there by an Indian when he was drunk.
He was a bad Indian, and they should have killed him too;
An Indian just now told me he is killed.
That's right.

Chippeway.

Nin gamárcha.
Shashy'yar kee bóossin nar négee?
Angáymer, pánimar tercúshin nin.
O, níshshishshin baskéyzegan árthty nar?
Angáymer.
Gar warbemór?
Maunder bowwískar.
Oway póckcan páyshik;
Maúnder páyshik O, níshshishshin indenéndum.
Ab'boy nee gúyyossay;
Oway páyshik.
Meegwotch, neecárnis.
Aúnday keen O, mentimóyey?
Sharshy'yar nepoo.
Maywísher nar?
Pa'yshik bebóne shy'yar.
Ar'thty O, jánis nogóme pemártus?
Páyshik oskenáygay áighter:
Géosay ween nar?
Kamarchy.
Aúnday chemayn?
Nee warbemór awáss bebóne woity Sheecark Sakíegan;
Páyshik níshinnorbay ojey gúnnissar ween osquíbby.
Ween O, mátchee níshinnórbay, meégwoyack O, gúnniesar ween gúyyea;
Shashy'yar ojey gúnnesar, ween nogóme me ecárto níshinnorbay;
Meegwoyack.

VOCABULARY.

English.

Was he old?
No.
He had three packs of beaver skins, and ten bags of dried meat, besides fish, when he was killed:
Oh! that was hard.
Who is that coming?
A strange Indian:
I will go and see him.
Are you come from far, friend?
No, a little way from hence.
What have you brought?
A small pack of beaver.
What will you want?
Blankets.
I have none but small for your children.
What is your trader's name at the Red Lake?

The Good Heart.
Has he many goods there?
Five large canoes full.
Have you any bears' grease?
One box only.
I will trade with you for it;
Very well, friend.
How many beaver skins did you give for that blanket?
Eleven.
I want to buy such;

VOCABULARY.

Chippeway.

Keewáency nar?
Cáwween.
Ween arthty neésswoy meekintárgan appimíniquy metósswoy múshcomat wéass spárchtay metách keegónce gúyyea:
Taw! waw! sannegat.
Hawwaneeyaw tercúshin?
Póckan Níshinno'rbay:
Nin eszar gar warbem'or.
Awássa nar kee tercúshin, neegee?
Cáwween, páyshew omar.
Wa'ygonin kee ogúbbetoon?
Hagúshenonce meekinta'rgan appimíniquy.
Wa'ygonin kee gúyyossay?
Wa'perwoyan.
Ca'wween kaygo wa'rpewoyan hagúshenonce kee janis shena'rgussey.
Ta'rnin sheneca'zeau keennerwind arta'wwaywinnin Misquíttyyang Sakíegna?
Níshshishshin oa'thty.
Nepewar huncúshigon a'rthty nar?
Na'rnan kítchee cheeman mo'oshquenay.
Mackqua'h pímmethy a'rthty nar?
Pa'yshik muccuck a'ighter.
Nee wee arta'wway;
Meégwoyack, négee.
An'dersoy appimíniquy kee, kee, arta'wway, wa'perwoyan?
Meto'sswoy asshea pa'yshik.
Nee wee arta'wway shenargussey;

VOCABULARY.

English.

You will get such at the English trader's.
How many beaver skins will you take for this?
Twenty:
Take them, friend.
Will you trade for those otter skins?
No, not now; I must pay my credit to the **Good Heart**.

What did you take from him?
Some small things.
Fetch me some water.
Make haste.
Do you hear me?
I hear you.
Come here;
I am coming.
What kind of a hunt had the *Fox* last winter?
The winter was bad indeed.
What did he hunt for?
Bear.
I wish this was spring, and all the Indians would come and trade their winter's hunt;
They will come soon:
I think they will have a great many packs.
What will you ask to take me by water from Montreal to Michilli-makinac?
One large keg of rum, one gun, one blanket, one kettle, and one knife; that is all I want:

VOCABULARY.
Chippeway.

Sa'ggonash a'rthty shena'rgussey.
An'dersoy appimíniquy kee tarpena'n mor?
Neesh tanner:
Tarpena'n neeca'rnis.
Cúnner kee wee arta'wway maúnder nekeék woygan?-
Cáwween, nogóme; nee wee gudderpa'rhan nee marseyna'ygan níshshishshin o'athty.
Wa'ygonin kee tarpena'n?
Póngay ka'ygoshish.
Nippee nartin.
Ha, webitta'n.
Cunner kee sto'otewar?
Kee, kee, no'neydone.
Onda'ss;
Nin tercúshin.
Ta'rnin shena'rgussey géosay *Assinbo* awa'ss bebo'ne?
Hapadgey ma'tchee bebo'ne.
Wa'ygonin ween géosay?
Mackqua'h.
Ba'dash meno'kemeg ha cockinno'r marmo níshinnorbay tercúshin ojey arta'wway awass bebo'ne O, wo'ygan;
Weeba'tch tercushin weénnewar:
Nepewar meekinta'rgan indenéndum weénnewar.
Wa'ygonin kee nindootymond monyny'yank woíty Michillima'kinac pamis'kian?
Pa'yshik kitchee muckcúck scotaywa'bo, pa'yshik baskéyzegan, payshik wa'perwoyan, pa'yshik akeek, pa'yshik mo'koman; me cockinno'r:

VOCABULARY.

English.

That is too much, as you will eat and drink the same as us, and will not work, but only shew the way.
Will you go directly?
No, I shall stay till to-morrow, and then embark.
I left my wife and children at a place four days march from hence.

I want to see them.
To-morrow, at the dawn of day, we will embark.
Take courage; farewell, friend.
Very well, I will be true to my word.
All is quiet.
I will go to bed.
Get up, friend.
I am lazy.
I am sick.
I am vexed.
I am cold.
I am hot.
I am hungry.
I am dry.
I am well.
I love you.
Your health, friend.
I do not understand you.

VOCABULARY.

Chippeway.

Ozo'me kee tabisco'ach wíssinnin neénnerwind mínniquy ca'wween a'r-wayyor kee gúsketoon meekan mee áighter unter wabindan'.

Weebatch gúddeszar keen?

Ca'wween, omar ojey appay; warbunk boossin.

Mee woity ojey appay, mentimóyamish, ja'nis woke, guyyea neon ogún-negat.

Nee, nee, warbema't weennewar.

Warbunk thurenscra boossin.

Hagua'rmissey, way, way, negee.

Meegwoyack, nee gar débwoy.

Súggermarch.

Péshshemo nin gama'rchar.

Goníshcar, neegee.

Kittim nin.

Acquoisee nin.

Nishcar'teseyan.

Geessénnar nin.

Geesha'rtay nin.

Bócketty nin.

Spa'rchtay nin.

Pema'rtissey nin.

Neeza'rgay keen.

Kee talleneman'co, or, kee tan'nemecó neejee.

Cawween nee stoticee.

THE END.

www.ingramcontent.com/pod-product-compliance
Lightning Source LLC
Chambersburg PA
CBHW021954220426
43663CB00007B/811